Informing the legislative debate since 1914 _____

Cuba: U.S. Restrictions on Travel and Remittances

Mark P. Sullivan
Specialist in Latin American Affairs

February 4, 2014

Congressional Research Service

7-5700

www.crs.gov

RL31139

Summary

Restrictions on travel to Cuba have been a key and often contentious component in U.S. efforts to isolate Cuba's communist government since the early 1960s. Under the George W. Bush Administration, restrictions on travel and on private remittances to Cuba were tightened. In March 2003, the Administration eliminated travel for people-to-people educational exchanges unrelated to academic coursework. In June 2004, the Administration further restricted family and educational travel, eliminated the category of fully-hosted travel, and restricted remittances so that they could only be sent to the remitter's immediate family. Initially there was mixed reaction to the Administration's June 2004 tightening of Cuba travel and remittance restrictions, but opposition to the policy grew, especially within the Cuban American community regarding the restrictions on family travel and remittances.

Obama Administration Policy

Under the Obama Administration, Congress took action in March 2009 by including two provisions in the FY2009 omnibus appropriations measure (P.L. 111-8) that eased restrictions on family travel and travel related to marketing and sale of agricultural and medical goods to Cuba. Subsequently, in April 2009, President Obama announced that his Administration would go further and allow unlimited family travel and remittances. Regulations implementing these changes were issued in September 2009. The new regulations also included the authorization of general licenses for travel transactions for telecommunications-related sales and for attendance at professional meetings related to commercial telecommunications.

In January 2011, the Obama Administration announced policy changes further easing restrictions on travel and remittances. The measures (1) increase purposeful travel to Cuba related to religious, educational, and people-to-people exchanges; (2) allow any U.S. person to send remittances to non-family members in Cuba and make it easier for religious institutions to send remittances for religious activities; and (3) permit all U.S. international airports to apply to provide services to licensed charter flights. These new measures, with the exception of the expansion of eligible airports, are similar to policies that were undertaken by the Clinton Administration in 1999, but subsequently curtailed by the Bush Administration in 2003-2004.

Legislative Initiatives

There were several attempts in the 112th Congress aimed at rolling back the Obama Administration's actions easing restrictions on travel and remittances, but none of these were approved. Several legislative initiatives were also introduced that would have further eased or lifted such restrictions altogether, but no action was taken on these measures.

In the 113th Congress, both the House and Senate versions of the FY2014 Financial Services and General Government appropriations measure, H.R. 2786 and S. 1371, had provisions that would have tightened and eased travel restrictions, respectively, but none of these provisions were included in the FY2014 omnibus appropriations measure, H.R. 3547 (P.L. 113-76), signed into law January 17, 2014. The House Appropriations Committee version of the bill, H.R. 2786 (H.Rept. 113-172), would have prohibited FY2014 funding used "to approve, license, facilitate, authorize, or otherwise allow" people-to-people travel to Cuba. In contrast, the Senate version of the measure, S. 1371(S.Rept. 113-80), would have expanded the current general license for professional research and meetings in Cuba to allow U.S. groups to sponsor and organize conferences in Cuba, but only if specifically related to disaster prevention, emergency preparedness, and natural resource protection.

As in past Congresses, several legislative initiatives again have been introduced that would lift all travel restrictions: H.R. 871 (Rangel) would lift travel restrictions; H.R. 873 (Rangel) would lift travel restrictions and restrictions on U.S. agricultural exports; and H.R. 214 (Serrano), H.R. 872 (Rangel), and H.R. 1917 would lift the overall embargo, including travel restrictions.

For further information, see CRS Report R43024, *Cuba: U.S. Policy and Issues for the 113th Congress*, by Mark P. Sullivan.

Contents

Appendixes

Contacts

Recent Developments

On January 17, 2014, President Obama signed into law the Consolidated Appropriations Act, 2014, H.R. 3547 (P.L. 113-76), which includes, as Division E, Financial Services and General Government Appropriations for FY2014. The measure does not include any provisions from the House or Senate Appropriations Committee versions of the FY2014 Financial Services and General Government Appropriations bills, H.R. 2786 (H.Rept. 113-172) and S. 1371 (S.Rept. 113-80), that would have tightened and eased restrictions on travel to Cuba respectively. H.R. 2786 had a provision in Section 124 that would have prohibited funding for any additional authorization of people-to-people exchanges during the fiscal year as well as a provision in Section 125 that would have required a Treasury Department report on specific information related to family travel to Cuba. S. 1371 had a provision in Section 628 that would have authorized a new general license for professional travel related to disaster prevention, emergency preparedness, and natural resource protection. (See "Legislative Initiatives in the 113th Congress" below.)

Overview of the U.S. Restrictions

Since the United States imposed a comprehensive trade embargo against Cuba in the early 1960s, there have been numerous policy changes to restrictions on travel to Cuba. The embargo regulations do not ban travel itself, but place restrictions on any financial transactions related to travel to Cuba, which effectively result in a travel ban. Accordingly, from 1963 until 1977, travel to Cuba was effectively banned under the Cuban Assets Control Regulations (CACR) issued by the Treasury Department's Office of Foreign Assets Control (OFAC) to implement the embargo. In 1977, the Carter Administration made changes to the regulations that essentially lifted the travel ban. In 1982, the Reagan Administration made other changes to the CACR that once again restricted travel to Cuba, but allowed for travel-related transactions by certain categories of travelers. Under the Clinton Administration, there were several changes to the Treasury Department regulations, with some at first tightening the restrictions, and others later loosening the restrictions.

Under the George W. Bush Administration, the travel regulations were tightened significantly, with additional restrictions on family visits, educational travel, and travel for those involved in amateur and semi-professional international sports federation competitions. In addition, the categories of fully-hosted travel and people-to-people educational exchanges unrelated to academic coursework were eliminated as permissible travel to Cuba. The Bush Administration also cracked down on those traveling to Cuba illegally, further restricted religious travel by changing licensing guidelines for such travel, and suspended the licenses of several travel service providers in Florida for license violations.

Under the Obama Administration, Congress took action in March 2009 (P.L. 111-8) to ease restrictions on travel by Cuban Americans to visit their family in Cuba and on travel related to the marketing and sale of agricultural and medical goods to Cuba. In April 2009, President Obama went even further by announcing that all restrictions on family travel and on remittances to family members in Cuba would be lifted, and on September 3, 2009, the Treasury Department issued regulations implementing these policy changes. In January 2011, President Obama took further action to ease restrictions on travel and remittances to Cuba by providing new general licenses for travel involving educational and religious activities and restoring a specific license authorizing travel for people-to-people exchanges. The Administration also restored a general license for any U.S. person to send remittances to Cuba (up to $500 per quarter) and created a general license for remittances to religious organizations. Finally, the Administration also expanded the U.S. airports eligible to provide services to flights to and from Cuba. In most respects, with the exception of the expansion of eligible airports, these new measures appear to be similar to policies that were undertaken by the Clinton Administration in 1999 but were subsequently curtailed by the Bush Administration in 2003 and 2004.

The President has the authority to ease restrictions on travel to Cuba. For example, the President could choose to authorize travel to Cuba under a general license for all eligible categories of travel. Lifting all the restrictions on travel, however, would require legislative action. This is because of the codification of the embargo in Section 102(h) of the Cuban Liberty and Democratic Solidarity Act of 1996 (P.L. 104-114); that act conditions the lifting of the embargo, including the travel restrictions, on the fulfillment of certain democratic conditions in Cuba. Although the Administration retains flexibility through licensing authority to ease travel restrictions, the President may not lift all restrictions on travel as set forth in the CACR. Moreover, a provision in the Trade Sanctions Reform and Export Enhancement Act of 2000 (§910(b) of P.L. 106-387, Title IX) prevents the Administration from licensing travel for tourist activities, and defines such activities as any activity not expressly authorized in the 12 broad categories of travel set forth in the CACR regulations. This legislative provision essentially circumscribes the authority of the executive branch to issue travel licenses for activities beyond the broad categories of travel allowed, and would have to be amended, superseded by new legislation, or repealed in order to expand categories of travel to Cuba or lift travel restrictions altogether.

June 2004 Tightening of Travel and Remittance Restrictions

There was mixed reaction to the Bush Administration's June 2004 tightening of Cuba travel and remittance restrictions, including within the Cuban American community. President Bush maintained that such restrictions would "prevent the regime from exploiting hard currency of tourists and remittances to Cubans to prop up their repressive regime."[1] Supporters of the tightened restrictions argued that both educational and family travel to Cuba had become fronts for tourist travel. Tightening up on such travel, they argued, would deny the regime dollars that help maintain its repressive control. (According to the Commission for Assistance for a Free Cuba, some 125,000 family visits to Cuba in 2003 resulted in about $96 million in hard currency for the government.)[2] Another argument made by some supporters of the tightened restrictions was that the limiting of family travel to once every three years would help ensure that such travel was limited to family emergencies. Along these lines, some argued that limiting family travel would make travelers more sensitive to political repression on the island and highlights that Cuban Americans are political refugees, not economic immigrants. Some supporters of the additional remittance restrictions argued that the Bush Administration demonstrated a continuation of the compassionate policy of supporting the Cuban people by not cutting the level of remittances allowed, $300 per quarter. They emphasized that the Administration only took

---

[1] President George W. Bush, "Remarks After Meeting with the Commission for Assistance for a Free Cuba," U.S. Department of State, May 6, 2004.

[2] Commission for Assistance to a Free Cuba, Report to the President, May 2004, p. 37.

action to ensure that the remittances would be restricted to immediate family members and not benefit certain members of the Cuban government and Cuban Communist Party.

Opponents of the tightened travel and remittance restrictions made a number of policy arguments. They maintained that the restrictions were anti-family and violated the basic principle of family reunification. Some in the Cuban American community argued that the policy of restricting family visits was inhumane and only resulted in more suffering for Cuban families. They especially opposed the additional restrictions that did not allow travel to visit cousins, aunts, uncles, and more-distant relatives. Another argument opposing restrictions on travel and private remittances was that the steps would have no effect on reducing repression in Cuba or weakening the government's instruments of repression. Opponents of the tightened restrictions maintained that the new restrictions were opposed by several prominent Cuban dissidents, including Oswaldo Payá of the Varela Project and Elizardo Sanchez of the Cuban Commission for Human Rights and National Reconciliation. Miriam Leiva, one of the founders of the Ladies in White human rights group, maintained that the policy punished dissidents and their families; she compared the U.S. restrictions to the situation faced by Cubans, who cannot travel without permission from the Cuban government.[3] Former political prisoner Oscar Espinosa Chepe, released from prison in December 2004, called the U.S. policy "absurd," maintaining that "what we need is to create space for dialogue."[4]

There were also concerns that the new restrictions were drafted without considering the full consequences of their implementation. For example, the elimination of the category of fully-hosted travel raised concerns about the status some 70 U.S. students receiving full scholarships at the Latin American School of Medicine in Havana. The school has more than 3,000 students from 23 countries and consists of a six-month pre-med program and a six-year medical school program. Members of the Congressional Black Caucus, who were instrumental in the establishment of the scholarship program for U.S. students, expressed concern that the students could have been forced to abandon their medical education because of the new OFAC regulations. As a result of these concerns, OFAC ultimately licensed the medical students to continue their studies and engage in travel-related transactions.

In the aftermath of the Bush Administration's tightening of travel restrictions, there was increased opposition to the policy and several groups were established opposing the Administration's actions. A group known as ENCASA, the Emergency Network of Cuban American Scholars and Artists for Change in Cuba Policy, launched a media campaign in 2006 opposing the travel restrictions.[5] In June 2006, another group of some 450 scholars known as the Emergency Coalition to Defend Educational Travel (ECDET) filed suit in U.S. federal court in Washington against the Treasury Department, maintaining that travel restrictions violated academic freedom.[6] (On November 4, 2008, the U.S. Court of Appeals for the District of Columbia found that the travel restrictions do not violate the right to academic freedom.)[7]

---

[3] Miriam Leiva, "Whose Country Is It, Anyway?" May 24, 2004, http://Salon.com; and "Why Deal with North Korea and Not Cuba," *Miami Herald*, March 1, 2008.

[4] David Adams, "Dissidents Say It's Time to Open Talks," *St Petersburg Times*, December 18, 2006.

[5] Oscar Corral, "Scholars, Artists Rip Embargo," *Miami Herald*, April 26, 2006.

[6] "Cuba's Campus Attrition," *CQ Weekly*, July 24, 2006; also see ECDET's website available at http://www.ecdet.org/.

[7] Jack Chang, "Court Upholds Limits on Student Trips to Cuba," *Miami Herald*, November 5, 2008.

With regard to family travel, a group in Miami, the Association of Christian Women in Defense of the Cuban Family, organized several protests against the tightened family travel restrictions.[8] In March 2008, Cuban Americans living in Vermont filed a complaint in U.S. federal court in Burlington, VT, that U.S. restrictions on family travel to Cuba violate their civil rights. Affiliates of the American Civil Liberties Union of Florida, Massachusetts, and Vermont subsequently filed a brief in support of the complaint. Human Rights Watch maintained that the U.S. travel policies inflicted harm on Cuban families and undermined the freedom of movement of hundreds of thousands of Cuban Americans.[9] In a 2005 report, Human Rights Watch cited numerous cases of family hardships after the tightened family travel restrictions went into effect, including the inability to visit children, sick or dying parents, or to attend funerals.[10]

A 2007 Florida International University poll examining attitudes of the Cuban American community in South Florida showed that about 64% of respondents wanted to return to the less restrictive policies on travel and remittances that were in place in 2003. Moreover, 55.2% of respondents supported allowing unrestricted travel overall, not just family travel.[11]

Easing of Restrictions in 2009

The tightening of family travel restrictions became an issue during the 2008 presidential campaign with candidate Barack Obama pledging to lift restrictions for family travel and remittances to Cuba.

With the election of Obama, the 111th Congress moved to ease family travel restrictions in March 2009 by approving two provisions that eased sanctions on travel to Cuba in FY2009 omnibus appropriations legislation (P.L. 111-8). Unlike the Bush Administration, the Obama Administration did not threaten to veto such legislation easing Cuba sanctions. This marked the first congressional action easing Cuba sanctions in almost a decade.

In the first provision, as implemented by the Treasury Department, family travel was again allowed once every 12 months under a general license to visit a close relative for an unlimited length of stay, and the limit for daily expenditure allowed by family travelers became the same as for other authorized travelers to Cuba (the State Department maximum per diem rate for Havana). The definition of "close relative" was expanded to mean any individual related to the traveler by blood, marriage, or adoption who is no more than three generations removed from that person.

The second provision in the omnibus measure required a general license for travel related to the marketing and sale of agricultural and medical goods to Cuba. The Treasury Department's Office of Foreign Assets Control ultimately issued regulations implementing this omnibus provision on September 3, 2009. The regulations require a written report at least 14 days before departure identifying both the traveler and the producer or distributor and describing the purpose and scope of such travel. Another written report is required within 14 days of return from Cuba describing the activities conducted, the persons met, and the expenses incurred. The regulations also require

---

[8] Laura Morales, "Protesters Call for Family-Friendly Cuban Travel," *Miami Herald*, August 27, 2006.

[9] Human Rights Watch, *World Report 2008*, January 2008.

[10] Human Rights Watch, Families Torn Apart, *The High Cost of U.S. and Cuban Travel Restrictions*, October 2005.

[11] "2007 FIU Cuba Poll," Institute for Public Opinion Research and Cuban Research Institute, Florida International University.

that such travelers under this provision be regularly employed by a producer or distributor of the agricultural commodities or medical products or an entity duly appointed to represent such a producer or distributor. The activity schedules for such travelers cannot include free time, travel, or recreation in excess of that consistent with a full work schedule.

Going even further, the Obama Administration announced several significant measures to ease U.S. sanctions on Cuba in April 2009. Fulfilling a campaign pledge, President Obama announced that all restrictions on family travel and on remittances to family members in Cuba would be lifted. This significantly superseded the action taken by Congress in March that had essentially reverted family travel restrictions to as they had been before they were tightened in 2004. Under the new policy announced by the Administration in April, there are no limitations on the frequency or duration of family visits (which would still be covered under a general license) and the 44-pound limitation on accompanied baggage was removed. Family travelers are allowed to spend the same as allowed for other travelers, up to the State Department's maximum per diem rate for Havana (which varies, but as of February 2014 was set at $188).[12] With regard to family remittances, the previous limitation of no more than $300 per quarter was removed with no restriction on the amount or frequency of the remittances. Authorized travelers were again authorized to carry up to $3,000 in remittances.[13] Regulations for the above policy changes were issued by the Treasury and Commerce Departments on September 3, 2009.

Easing of Restrictions in 2011

On January 14, 2011, the Obama Administration announced a series of policy changes further easing restrictions on travel and remittances to Cuba that had been rumored in the second half of 2010. The changes are designed to make it easier to engage in educational, religious, and other types of people-to-people travel and allow all Americans to send remittances to Cuba. The changes are similar to policy that was in place from 1999 under the Clinton Administration through mid-2004 under the Bush Administration. President Obama directed the Secretaries of State, Treasury, and Homeland Security to amend regulations and policies "in order to continue efforts reach out to the Cuban people in support of their desire to freely determine their country's future."[14] The Administration maintains that the policy changes will increase people-to-people contact, help strengthen Cuban civil society, and make Cuban people less dependent on the Cuban state.[15] The changes occurred at the same time that the Cuban government began laying off thousands of state workers and increasing private enterprise through an expansion of the authorized categories for self-employment.

According to the White House announcement, the policy changes would be enacted through modifications to existing regulations. This occurred on January 28, 2011, when the Departments of the Treasury and Homeland Security published changes to the regulations in the *Federal Register*.[16]

---

[12] See U.S. Department of State, Foreign Per Diem Rates by Location, available at http://aoprals.state.gov/web920/per_diem.asp.

[13] White House, "Fact Sheet: Reaching Out to the Cuban People," April 13, 2009.

[14] White House, Office of the Press Secretary, "Reaching Out to the Cuban People," January 14, 2011, available at http://www.whitehouse.gov/the-press-office/2011/01/14/reaching-out-cuban-people.

[15] Mary Beth Sheridan, "Obama Loosens Travel Restrictions to Cuba," *Washington Post*, January 15, 2011.

[16] U.S. Department of the Treasury, "Cuban Assets Control Regulations," Vol. 76, No. 19 *Federal Register* 5072-5078, (continued...)

The measures (1) increase purposeful travel to Cuba related to religious, educational, and journalistic activities (general licenses are now authorized for certain types of educational and religious travel; people-to-people travel exchanges are authorized via a specific license); (2) allow any U.S. person to send remittances to non-family members in Cuba and make it easier for religious institutions to send remittances for religious activities (general licenses are now authorized for both); and (3) allow all U.S. international airports to apply to provide services to licensed charter flights to and from Cuba. In most respects, these new measures appear to be similar to policies that were undertaken by the Clinton Administration in 1999, but were subsequently curtailed by the Bush Administration in 2003 and 2004. An exception is the expansion of airports to service licensed flights to and from Cuba. While the new travel regulations immediately went into effect for those categories of travel falling under a general license category, OFAC delayed processing applications for new travel categories requiring a specific license (such as people-to-people exchanges) until it updated and issued guidelines.[17] These ultimately were issued in April 2011: *Comprehensive Guidelines for License Applications to Engage in Travel-related Transactions Involving Cuba.*[18]

- **Purposeful Travel**. With regard to purposeful travel, the policy changes allowed religious organizations to sponsor religious travel to Cuba under a general license as opposed to the previous requirement for a specific license for such travel. Restrictions on educational travel were eased in several ways: educational travel for academic credit is now allowed under a general license (instead of a specific license as previously required); students are now allowed to participate through academic institutions other than their own; and instructor support is allowed from adjunct and part-time staff. Academic institutions are allowed to apply for specific licenses to sponsor or cosponsor academic seminars, conferences, and workshops related to Cuba and allow faculty, staff, and students to attend. People-to-people exchanges, under the auspices of an organization that sponsors and organizes such programs, are now allowed under a specific license (such activities previously had been allowed from 1999-2003).

- **Remittances**. The policy changes restored a general license category available for any U.S. person to send up to $500 in remittances per quarter to non-family members in Cuba (but not to senior Cuban government officials or senior members of the Cuban Communist Party) to support private economic activity, among other purposes. A general license also was created for remittances to religious institutions in Cuba in support of religious activities.

- **U.S. Airports**. The policy changes expanded the number of eligible airports in the United States authorized to serve licensed charter flights to

(...continued)

January 28, 2011; Department of Homeland Security, "Airports of Entry or Departure for Flights to and from Cuba," Vol. 76, No. 19 *Federal Register* 5058-5061, January 28, 2011.

[17] CRS correspondence with the Treasury Department, March 17, 2011.

[18] The guidelines were subsequently revised again in May 2012. See U.S. Department of the Treasury, Office of Foreign Assets Control, *Comprehensive Guidelines for License Applications to Engage in Travel-related Transactions Involving Cuba*, May 10, 2012, available at http://www.treasury.gov/resource-center/sanctions/Programs/Documents/cuba_tr_app.pdf.

and from Cuba. The Clinton Administration had expanded airports eligible to service license charter flights beyond that of Miami International Airport to international airports in Los Angeles and New York (JFK) in 1999, but the January 2011 policy change allows all U.S. international airports to apply to provide services for chartered flights to and from Cuba under certain conditions. The airport would need to have adequate customs and immigration capabilities, and a licensed travel service provider would need to have expressed an interest in providing service to and from Cuba from the airport. (Currently there are 19 U.S. airports authorized by U.S. Customs and Border Protection to serve licensed flights to and from Cuba, although not all provide such service. In addition, to JFK, Miami, and Los Angeles, the other authorized airports are Atlanta, Austin (Texas), Baltimore-Washington (BWI), Chicago O'Hare, Dallas-Fort Worth, Fort Lauderdale-Hollywood, Houston, Key West, New Orleans, Oakland (California), Orlando, Palm Beach, Pittsburgh, San Juan (Puerto Rico), Southwest Florida International Airport (Fort Myers), and Tampa.[19] Being on the authorization list, however, does not necessarily mean that airlines will offer flights from these airports. It is a matter of economic feasibility for the air charter companies. As of early 2014, air charter companies were only operating flights from Florida, largely from Miami, but also from Tampa and Fort Lauderdale.[20])

By early July 2011, OFAC confirmed that it had approved the first licenses for U.S. people-to-people organizations to bring U.S. visitors to Cuba, and the first such trips began in August 2011.[21] On July 25, 2011, however, prior to the trips beginning, OFAC issued an advisory maintaining that misstatements in the media had suggested that U.S. policy now allows for virtually unrestricted group travel to Cuba, and reaffirmed that travel conducted by people-to-people travel groups licensed for travel to Cuba must "certify that all participants will have a full-time schedule of educational exchange activities that will result in meaningful interaction between the travelers and individuals in Cuba." The advisory stated that authorized activities by people-to-people groups are not "tourist activities," and pointed out that the Trade Sanctions Reform and Export Enhancement Act of 2000 prohibits OFAC from licensing transactions for tourist activities.[22]

Policy groups in favor of increased U.S. engagement with Cuba largely praised the Administration's action as a significant step forward in reforming U.S.-Cuban relations and as an important means to expand the flow of information and ideas to Cuba and to increase the income of Cubans working in the expanding private sector. Perhaps more surprisingly, the Miami-based

---

[19] U.S. Department of Homeland Security, Customs and Border Protection, "Technical Amendment to Cuba Airport List: Addition of Recently Approved Airport," *Federal Register*, April 20, 2012, pp. 23598-23599.

[20] Mimi Whitefield, "Cuba Charter Business Consolidates in Florida," *Miami Herald*, January 5, 2014.

[21] Peter Orsi, "U.S. Licensing Travel Operators to Start Up Legal Cuba Trips, Treasury Department Says," *Associated Press*, July 1, 2011; Mimi Whitefield, "People-to-People Tours to Cuba Take Off Thursday," *Miami Herald*, August 10, 2011; and Jeff Franks, "Purposeful Cuba Trips Resume," *Chicago Tribune*, August 18, 2011. Also see the following online resource: *Organizations Sponsoring People-to-People Travel to Cuba*, Latin America Working Group Education Fund, available at http://www.lawg.org/storage/documents/people2people.pdf.

[22] U.S. Department of the Treasury, OFAC, "Cuba Travel Advisory," July 25, 2011, available at http://www.treasury.gov/resource-center/sanctions/Programs/Documents/cuba_trav_adv.pdf.

Cuban American National Foundation (CANF) strongly supported the Administration's policy changes. According to CANF President Francisco "Pepe" Hernández: "A greater ability to send remittances in conjunction with increased contact and communication with those on the island will help to break the chains of dependency that the Castro regime has used to oppress those inside Cuba."[23]

In contrast, policy groups opposed to easing U.S. sanctions criticized the Administration, maintaining that the policy changes would help prop up Cuba's repressive government when it was most vulnerable because of the difficult economic situation. Opponents of the policy changes argued that sending dollars via increased travel by Americans and increased remittances would help the Cuban government maintain in place its repressive policies. They also argued that easing the restrictions on travel and remittances would not bring about respect for human rights in Cuba.

The Cuban government characterized the U.S. policy changes as positive, but maintained that they were limited in scope and did not alter policy toward Cuba. A statement by Cuba's Ministry of Foreign Affairs maintained that the policy changes did not restore the right to travel to Cuba for all American citizens, and that the United States should lift the blockade (embargo) and the prohibition on travel to Cuba if it is interested in expanding and facilitating contacts between Cubans and Americans.[24]

In the first session of the 112th Congress, there were several attempts aimed at rolling back the Obama Administration's actions easing restrictions on travel and remittances, including a provision originating in the House Appropriation Committee's version of the FY2012 Financial Services and General Government appropriations measure, H.R. 2434. The White House had threatened to veto the bill if it contained the provision, and stood firm when congressional leaders were considering including the provision in a "megabus" FY2012 appropriations bill, H.R. 2055. Ultimately congressional leaders agreed not to include the provision in the appropriations measure (P.L. 112-74). (See "Legislative Initiatives in the 112th Congress" below.)

Developments in 2012

In 2012, some Members of Congress expressed concerns about people-to-people travel that appeared to be focusing on tourist activities rather than on purposeful travel. In response, the Treasury Department issued an announcement in March 2012 warning about misleading advertising regarding some people-to-people trips that could lead to OFAC investigating the organization conducting the trips. The announcement maintained that licenses could be revoked and that organizations may be issued a civil penalty up to $65,000 per violation.[25] OFAC followed up this announcement in May 2012 by revising its people-to-people license guidelines. The revised guidelines reflect similar language to the March announcement and also require an organization applying for a people-to-people license to describe how the travel "would enhance contact with the Cuban people, and/or support civil society in Cuba, and/or promote the Cuban

---

[23] Cuban American National Foundation, Press Release, "Cuban American National Foundation Supports New Cuba Policy Measures," January 14, 2011.

[24] Republic of Cuba, Ministry of Foreign Affairs, "Statement by the Ministry of Foreign Affairs," January 14, 2011.

[25] U.S. Department of the Treasury, OFAC, "Advertising Educational Exchange Travel to Cuba for People-to-People Contact," March 9, 2012, available at http://www.treasury.gov/resource-center/sanctions/Programs/Pages/cuba_ppl_notice.aspx.

people's independence from Cuban authorities."[26] (For more details, see "Chronology of Cuba Travel Restrictions" below.)

On April 27, 2012, a suspicious fire destroyed the Coral Gables, FL, office of Airline Brokers, a travel agency specializing in flights to Cuba. The Coral Gables fire department subsequently determined the fire to be caused by arson. The Federal Bureau of Investigation and the Bureau of Alcohol, Tobacco, Firearms, and Explosives became involved in the investigation of the fire.[27]

In June 7, 2012, congressional testimony, Assistant Secretary of State for Western Hemisphere Affairs Roberta Jacobson set forth a clear-cut description of U.S. policy toward Cuba in which she expressed strong U.S. support for democracy and human rights activists in Cuba and defended the Obama's Administration policy on travel and remittances. The Assistant Secretary asserted that "the Obama Administration's priority is to empower Cubans to freely determine their own future." She maintained that "the most effective tool we have for doing that is building connections between the Cuban and American people, in order to give Cubans the support and tools they need to move forward independent of their government." The Assistant Secretary maintained that "the Administration's travel, remittance and people-to-people policies are helping Cubans by providing alternative sources of information, taking advantage of emerging opportunities for self-employment and private property, and strengthening civil society."[28]

In September 2012, various press reports cited a slowdown in the Treasury Department's approval or reapproval of licenses for people-to-people travel since the agency had issued new guidelines in May (described above). Companies conducting such programs complained that the delay in the licenses was forcing them to cancel trips and even to lay off staff.[29] By early October 2012, however, companies conducting the people-to-people travel maintained that they were once again receiving license approvals.

Developments in 2013

In early April 2013, some Members of Congress strongly criticized singers Beyoncé Knowles-Carter and her husband Shawn Carter, better known as Jay-Z, for traveling to Cuba. Members were concerned that the trip, as described in the press, was primarily for tourism, which would be contrary to U.S. law and regulations. The Treasury Department stated that the two singers were participating in an authorized people-to-people exchange trip organized by a group licensed by OFAC to conduct such trips (pursuant to 31 CFR 515.565(b)(2) of the Cuban Assets Control Regulations). Some Members also criticized the singers for not meeting with those who have been oppressed by the Cuban government.

---

[26] U.S. Department of the Treasury, OFAC, "Comprehensive Guidelines for License Applications to Engage in Travel-Related Transactions Involving Cuba," Revised May 10, 2012, available at http://www.treasury.gov/resource-center/sanctions/Programs/Documents/cuba_tr_app.pdf

[27] Federal Bureau of Investigation, Miami Division, "FBI Release Photographs of a Vehicle of Interest in Connection with Coral Gables Fire," Press Release, June 7, 2012.

[28] Testimony of Roberta S. Jacobson, Assistant Secretary of State for Western Hemisphere Affairs, Senate Foreign Relations Committee, Subcommittee on Western Hemisphere, Peace Corps, and Global Narcotics, at a hearing entitled "The Path to Freedom: Countering Repression and Strengthening Civil Society," June 7, 2012, available at http://www.state.gov/p/wha/rls/rm/2012/191935 htm.

[29] Damien Cave, "Licensing Rules Slow Tours to Cuba," *New York Times*, September 16, 2012; Paul Haven, "U.S. Travel Outfits Say Rules for Legal Travel to Cuba Getting Tighter," *Associated Press*, September 13, 2012.

On April 30, 2013, 59 House Democrats sent a letter to President Obama lauding the President for his 2009 action lifting restrictions on family travel and remittances, and for his 2011 action easing restrictions on some categories of travel, including people-to-people travel. The Members also called for the President to further use his "executive authority to allow all current categories of permissible travel, including people-to-people travel," to be carried out under a general license (instead of having to apply to Treasury Department for a specific license). Such an action, according to the Members, would increase opportunities for engagement and help Cubans create more jobs and opportunities to expand their independence from the Cuban government.

In July 2013, the House and Senate Appropriations Committees reported out their versions of the FY2014 Financial Services and General Government appropriations measure, H.R. 2786 and S. 1371, with different provisions regarding U.S. policy on travel to Cuba. The House version would have tightened restrictions on travel by prohibiting funding for any additional authorization of people-to-people exchanges during the fiscal year, while the Senate version would have eased restrictions on travel by authorizing a new general license for professional travel related to disaster prevention, emergency preparedness, and natural resource protection. Ultimately, none of these provisions were included in the FY2014 omnibus appropriations measure, H.R. 3547 (P.L. 113-76), signed into law January 17, 2014. (For more details, see "Legislative Initiatives in the 113th Congress" below.)

Chronology of Cuba Travel Restrictions

1960—In the first trade restrictions on Cuba after the rise to power of Fidel Castro, President Eisenhower placed most U.S. exports to Cuba under validated license controls, except for nonsubsidized food, medicines, and medical supplies. The action did not include restrictions on travel.

1962/1963—In February 1962, President Kennedy imposed a trade embargo on Cuba because of the Castro government's ties to the Soviet Union. Pursuant to the President's directive, the Department of the Treasury's Office of Foreign Assets Control (OFAC) issued the Cuban Import Regulations. On July 9, 1963, OFAC issued a more comprehensive set of prohibitions, the Cuban Assets Control Regulations, which effectively banned travel by prohibiting any transactions with Cuba.

1977—In March, the Carter Administration announced the lifting of restrictions on U.S. travel to Cuba that had been in place since the early 1960s. The Carter Administration lifted the travel ban by issuing a general license for travel-related transactions for those visiting Cuba. Direct flights were also allowed.

1982—In April, the Reagan Administration reimposed restrictions on travel to Cuba, although it allowed for certain categories of travel, including travel by U.S. government officials, employees of news or filmmaking organizations, persons engaging in professional research, or persons visiting their close relatives. It did not allow for ordinary tourist or business travel that had been allowed since the Carter Administration's 1977 action.

1984—On June 28, the Supreme Court, in a 5-4 decision in the case of *Regan v. Wald*, rejected a challenge to the ban on travel to Cuba and asserted the executive branch's right to impose travel restrictions for national security reasons.

1993—The Clinton Administration, in June 1993, slightly amended restrictions on U.S. travel to Cuba. Two additional categories of travel were allowed: travel to Cuba "for clearly defined educational or religious activities"; and travel "for activities of recognized human rights organizations." In both categories, travelers were required to apply for a specific license from OFAC.

1994—In August, President Clinton announced several measures against the Cuban government in response to an escalation in the number of Cubans fleeing to the United States. Among these measures, the Administration tightened travel restrictions by prohibiting family visits under a general license, and allowing specific licenses for family visits only "when extreme hardship is demonstrated in cases involving extreme humanitarian need" such as terminal illness or severe medical emergency. Such visits required a specific license from OFAC. In addition, professional researchers were required to apply for a specific license, whereas since 1982 they had been able to travel freely under a general license. (*Federal Register*, August 30, 1994, pp. 44884-44886.)

1995—In October, President Clinton announced measures to ease some U.S. restrictions on travel and other activities with Cuba, with the overall objective of promoting democracy and the free flow of ideas. The new measures included authorizing general licenses for transactions relating to travel to Cuba for Cuban Americans making yearly visits to close relatives in "circumstances that demonstrate extreme humanitarian need." This reversed the August 1994 action that required specific licenses. However, those traveling for this purpose more than once in a 12-month period would need to apply to OFAC for a specific license. In addition, the new measures allowed for specific licenses for free-lance journalists traveling to Cuba. (*Federal Register*, October 20, 1995, pp. 54194-54198.)

1996—On February 26, following the shootdown of two U.S. civilian planes two days earlier by Cuban fighter jets, President Clinton took several measures against Cuba, including the indefinite suspension of charter flights between Cuba and the United States. Qualified licensed travelers could go to Cuba, provided their flights were routed through third countries.

1998—On March 20, following Pope John Paul II's January trip to Cuba, President Clinton announced several changes in U.S. policy toward Cuba, including the resumption of licensing for direct charter flights to Cuba. On July 2, OFAC issued licenses to nine air charter companies to provide direct passenger flights from Miami International Airport to Havana's José Martí International Airport.

1999—On January 5, President Clinton announced several measures to support the Cuban people that were intended to augment changes implemented in March 1998. Among the measures introduced was the expansion of direct passenger charter flights from additional U.S. cities other than Miami. In August, the State Department announced that direct flights to Cuba would be allowed from New York and Los Angeles. In addition, President Clinton also announced in January 1999 that measures would be taken to increase people-to-people exchanges. As a result, on May 13, 1999, OFAC issued a number of changes to the Cuba embargo regulations that effectively loosened restrictions on certain categories of travelers to Cuba. Travel for professional research became possible under a general license, and travel for a wide range of educational, religious, sports competition, and other activities became possible with specific licenses authorized by OFAC on a case-by-case basis. In addition, those traveling to Cuba to visit a close family member under either a general or specific license only needed to "demonstrate humanitarian need," as opposed to "extreme humanitarian need" that had been required since 1995. (*Federal Register*, May 13, 1999, pp. 25808-25820.)

2000—In October, Congress approved and the President signed the Trade Sanctions Reform and Export Enhancement Act of 2000 (Title IX of P.L. 106-387), which included a provision that prohibited travel-related transactions for "tourist activities," which as set forth in Section 910(b)(2) of the act are defined as any activity not authorized or referenced in the existing travel regulations (31 CFR 515.560, paragraphs (1) through (12)). The congressional action appeared to circumscribe the authority of the OFAC to issue specific travel licenses on a case-by-case basis that do not fit neatly within the categories of travel already allowed by the regulations.

2001—On July 12, OFAC published regulations pursuant to the provisions of the Trade Sanctions and Export Enhancement Act of 2000 (Title IX of P.L. 106-387) that prohibited travel-related transactions for "tourist activities." (*Federal Register*, July 12, 2001, pp. 36683-36688.) On July 13, 2001, President Bush announced that he had asked the Treasury Department to enhance and expand the capabilities of OFAC to prevent, among other things, "unlicensed and excessive travel."

2003—On January 29, OFAC published proposed enforcement guidelines (as an appendix to 31 CFR Part 501) for all its economic sanctions programs and additional guidelines (as an appendix to 31 CFR Part 515) for the Cuba sanctions program. The general guidelines provided a procedural framework for OFAC's enforcement of economic sanctions, while the Cuba-specific guidelines consist of penalties for different embargo violations. (*Federal Register*, January 29, 2003, pp. 4422-4429.)

On March 24, 2003, OFAC announced that the Cuba travel regulations were being amended to ease travel to Cuba for those visiting close relatives. (*Federal Register*, March 24, 2003, pp. 14141-14148.) Travel was permitted to visit relatives to within three degrees of relationship of the traveler and was not restricted to travel in circumstances of humanitarian need. The new regulations also increased the amount a traveler may carry, up to $3,000 (compared to $300 previously), although the limit of $300 per quarter destined for each household remained. Finally, the regulations were tightened for certain types of educational travel. People-to-people educational exchanges unrelated to academic coursework were no longer allowed. Some groups lauded the restriction of these educational exchanges because they believed they had become an opportunity for unrestricted travel; others criticized the Bush Administration's decision to restrict the second largest category of travel to Cuba in which ordinary people were able to travel and exchange with their counterparts on the island.

On October 10, 2003, President Bush instructed the Department of Homeland Security, as part of a broader initiative on Cuba, to increase inspections of travelers and shipments to and from Cuba in order to more strictly enforce the trade and travel embargo.

2004—On February 26, President Bush ordered the Department of Homeland Security to expand its policing of the waters between Florida and Cuba with the objective of stopping pleasure boating traffic. (*Federal Register*, March 1, 2004, pp. 9315-9517.)

On June 16, 2004, OFAC published changes to the CACR implementing the President's directives to implement certain recommendations of the Commission for Assistance to a Free Cuba. The new regulations tightened travel restrictions in several ways. Fully-hosted travel was eliminated as a legal category of permissible travel. Family visits were restricted to one trip every three years under a specific license to visit only immediate family (grandparents, grandchildren, parents, siblings, spouses, and children) for a period not to exceed 14 days. The daily amount of money that family visitors could spend while in Cuba was reduced from the State Department per diem rate for Havana (then $179) to $50. Specific licenses for visiting non-Cuban nationals in Cuba (such as a student) were limited to when the family member visited was in "exigent circumstances." The general license for amateur or semi-professional athletic teams to travel to Cuba to engage in sports competitions was eliminated; such travel now required a specific license. (*Federal Register*, June 16, 2004, pp. 33768-33774)

Specific licenses for educational activities were further restricted in several ways: the institutional licenses were restricted to undergraduate and graduate institutions, while the category of educational exchanges sponsored by secondary schools was eliminated; the duration of institutional licenses was shortened from two to one year; three types of licensed educational activities—structural education programs in Cuba offered as part of a course at the licensed institution; formal courses of study offered at a Cuban academic institution; and teaching at a Cuban academic institution—were required to be no shorter than 10 weeks.

The new regulations also further restricted sending cash remittances to Cuba. Quarterly remittances of $300 could still be sent, but were restricted to members of the remitter's immediate family and could not be remitted to certain government officials and certain members of the Cuban Communist Party. The regulations were also changed to reduce the amount of remittances that authorized travelers may carry to Cuba, from $3,000 to $300. This reversed OFAC's March 2003 changes to the regulations that had increased the amount that authorized travelers could carry to $3,000.

On June 22, 2004, the Department of Commerce's Bureau of Industry and Security (BIS) published regulations related to the recommendations of the Commission for Assistance to a Free Cuba. The new regulations placed new limits on gift parcels sent to Cuba and personal baggage of travelers going to Cuba. Gift parcels could no longer contain items such as seeds, clothing, personal hygiene items, veterinary medicines and supplies, fishing equipment and supplies, and soap-making equipment. Baggage was limited to 44 pounds. (*Federal Register*, pp. 34565-34567)

On July 8, 2004, the U.S. Coast Guard published regulations requiring U.S. vessels less than 100 meters to have a Coast Guard permit to enter Cuban territorial waters. (*Federal Register*, pp. 41367-41374)

2005—On March 31, OFAC made changes to its guidelines for license applications related to religious travel. According to the guidelines, specific licenses issued under CFR 515.566(b) for religious organizations only authorized up to 25 individuals to travel to Cuba no more than once per calendar quarter. The specific licenses under this section would not be valid for more than one year. (OFAC, *Comprehensive Guidelines for License Applications to Engage in Travel-related Transactions Involving Cuba*, Revised September 2004, p. 40, the relevant paragraph was updated March 31, 2005).

2009—On March 11, President Obama signed into law the Omnibus Appropriations Act, 2009 (P.L. 111-8), with two provisions easing restrictions on travel to Cuba.

Section 620 of Division D amended the Trade Sanctions Reform and Export Enhancement Act of 2000 (TSRA) to require the Secretary of the Treasury to issue regulations for travel to, from, or within Cuba under a general license for the marketing and sale of agricultural and medical goods, meaning that there would be no requirement to obtain special permission from OFAC. Such travel had required a specific license from OFAC, issued on a case-by-case basis. OFAC maintained that it would issue regulations in the coming weeks, although a letter from Secretary of the Treasury

Timothy Geithner published in the *Congressional Record* stated that the new regulations "would provide that the representatives of only a narrow class of businesses would be eligible, under a new general license, to travel to market and sell agricultural and medical goods." The Secretary also maintained that "any business using the general license would be required to provide both advance written notice outlining the purpose and scope of the planned travel and, upon return, a report outlining the activities conducted, including the persons with whom they met, the expenses incurred, and business conducted in Cuba." (*Congressional Record*, March 10, 2009, p. S2933.)

Section 621 of Division D prohibited funds from being used to administer, implement, or enforce family travel restrictions that were imposed by the Bush Administration in June 2004. OFAC implemented this provision by reinstating a general license for family travel as it existed prior to the Bush Administration's tightening of restrictions in June 2004. As implemented by OFAC, travel was allowed once every 12 months to visit a close relative for an unlimited length of stay, and the limit for daily expenditure allowed by family travelers became the same as for other authorized travelers to Cuba (State Department maximum per diem rate for Havana in effect when the travel takes place.) The new general license also expanded the definition of "close relative" to mean any individual related to the traveler by blood, marriage, or adoption who was no more than three generations removed from that person.

On April 13, 2009, President Obama directed that all restrictions on family travel and on remittances to family members in Cuba be lifted. The Administration also announced measures to expand the scope of eligible humanitarian donations through gift parcels and to increase telecommunications links with Cuba. (See the White House fact sheet available at http://www.whitehouse.gov/the_press_office/Fact-Sheet-Reaching-out-to-the-Cuban-people/.)

On September 3, 2009, OFAC issued amendments to the Cuban Assets Control Regulations implementing President Obama's policy changes with regard to family travel, remittances, and greater telecommunications links with Cuba. The amendments also included new categories of travel under general licenses, including travel for the marketing and sale of agricultural and medical goods (implementing the legislative provision approved in March 2009 described above) and travel for telecommunications providers and those attending professional meetings for commercial telecommunications transactions. (*Federal Register*, September 8, 2009, pp. 46000-46007.) On the same day, the Department of Commerce's Bureau of Industry and Security issued amendments to the Export Administration Regulations that expanded the value and list of eligible item that may be included in gift parcels to Cuba and removed the previous weight limit of 44 pounds for accompanied baggage to Cuba. (*Federal Register*, September 8, 2009, pp. 45985-45990.)

2011—On January 14, the White House announced that President Obama had directed the Secretaries of State, Treasury, and Homeland Security to make changes to regulations and policies to (1) increase purposeful travel to Cuba related to religious, educational, and journalistic activities; (2) allow any U.S. person to send remittances to non-family members in Cuba and make it easier for religious institutions to send remittances for religious activities; and (3) allow all U.S. international airports to provide services to licensed charter flights to and from Cuba. (See the White House statement at http://www.whitehouse.gov/the-press-office/2011/01/14/reaching-out-cuban-people.)

On January 28, 2011, OFAC issued changes to the CACR implementing the revised policy announced by the President on January 14 and designed to increase purposeful travel and ease restrictions on remittances to non-family members in Cuba and to religious institutions for religious activities (Federal Register, January 28, 2011, pp. 5072-5078). On the same day, the Department of Homeland Security (DHS), U.S. Customs and Border Protection (CBP), issued changes to DHS regulations to allow additional international airports in the United States to request approval of CBP to process authorized flights between the United States and Cuba (Federal Register, January 28, 2011, pp. 5058-5061).

On April 21, 2011, OFAC issued revised guidelines for travel license applications reflecting the policy changes set forth in January 2011. (U.S. Department of the Treasury, OFAC, Comprehensive Guidelines for License Applications to Engage in Travel-related Transactions Involving Cuba, Revised April 19, 2011.)

On July 25, 2011, OFAC issued an advisory reaffirming that travel conducted by people-to-people travel groups licensed for travel to Cuba must "certify that all participants will have a full-time schedule of educational exchange activities that will result in meaningful interaction between the travelers and individuals in Cuba." (U.S. Department of the Treasury, OFAC, "Cuba Travel Advisory," July 25, 2011)

2012—On March 9, 2012, OFAC published an announcement regarding advertising for people-to-people travel, noting that all advertisements must state the name of the licensed organization conducting the travel and that the organization must use the name under which their OFAC travel was licensed unless the group requests and receives a license amendment from OFAC to use an alternative name. The announcement also stated that advertising that appeared to suggest that the people-to-people trips were focused on activities that travelers may undertake off hours (after their daily full-time schedule of people-to-people activities) may give an incorrect impression and prompt OFAC to contact the licensed organization and conduct an investigation. It maintained that people-to-people organizations that failed to meet requirements of their licenses may have their licenses revoked or be issued a civil penalty up to $65,000 per violation. (U.S. Department of the Treasury, OFAC, "Advertising Educational Exchange Travel to Cuba for People-to-People Contact," March 9, 2012, available at http://www.treasury.gov/resource-center/sanctions/Programs/Pages/cuba_ppl_notice.aspx.)

On May 10, 2012, OFAC tightened restrictions on people-to-people travel by making changes to its license guidelines. The revised guidelines reflect similar language to the March 2012 announcement described above regarding advertising. The revised guidelines also require an organization applying for a people-to-people license to describe how the travel "would enhance contact with the Cuban people, and/or support civil society in Cuba, and/or promote the Cuban people's independence from Cuban authorities." Just as in 2011, the guidelines require applicants to certify that the predominant portion of activities engaged in will not be with prohibited Cuban government or Cuban Communist Party officials (as defined in 31 CFR 515.337 and 31 CFR 515.338), but the changes in May 2012 require that the sample itinerary for the proposed travel needs to specify how meetings with such officials advance purposeful travel by enhancing contact with the Cuban people, supporting civil society, or promoting independence from Cuban authorities (U.S. Department of the Treasury, OFAC, *Comprehensive Guidelines for License Applications to Engage in Travel-Related Transactions Involving Cuba*, Revised May 10, 2012).

Current Permissible Travel to Cuba

At present, certain categories of travelers may travel to Cuba under a *general* license, which means that there is no need to obtain special permission from OFAC. Nevertheless, those individuals traveling under a general license must be able to document that their travel qualifies under a general license, and must keep records for a period of five years after the travel transactions take place. Those eligible for travel under a general license include those visiting close relatives in Cuba; full-time journalists; full-time professionals conducting professional research (of a noncommercial, academic nature) or attending conferences sponsored by international professional organizations or associations; faculty, staff, and students of accredited U.S. graduate and undergraduate degree-making institutions engaged in one of several categories of educational activities in Cuba; members and staff of religious organizations engaged in a full-time program of in religious activities; and travel related to licensed sales of agricultural, medical, and telecommunications products.

In addition, a wide variety of travelers engaging in educational, religious, and humanitarian activities and people-to-people exchanges may be eligible for *specific* licenses. Applications for *specific* licenses are reviewed and granted by OFAC on a case-by-case basis. Some specific licenses may authorize multiple trips to Cuba over an extended period of time. Applicants for specific license have to wait for OFAC to issue the license prior to engaging in travel-related transactions.

The travel regulations can be found at 31 CFR 515.560, which references other sections of the Cuban Assets Control Regulations (CACR) for travel-related transaction licensing criteria. In addition, OFAC publishes *Comprehensive Guidelines for License Applications to Engage in Travel-related Transactions Involving Cuba*, which were most recently revised in May 2012, and a *List of Authorized Providers of Air, Travel and Remittance Forwarding Services to Cuba*, most recently revised in June 2013.[30]

While the U.S. government does not collect data on the overall number of Americans traveling to Cuba,[31] the Department of Transportation (DOT) collects statistics on the number of passengers on direct flights from the United States to Cuba. According to DOT statistics, there were almost 195,000 passengers on direct flights from the United States to Cuba in 2009, while the number rose to almost 242,000 in 2010, over 348,000 in 2011, and almost 357,000 in 2012.[32] These

---

[30] See OFAC's web page on Cuba Sanctions, available at http://www.treasury.gov/resource-center/sanctions/Programs/pages/cuba.aspx. OFAC's *Comprehensive Guidelines for License Applications to Engage in Travel-Related Transactions Involving Cuba*, revised May 10, 2012, is available at http://www.treasury.gov/resource-center/sanctions/Programs/Documents/cuba_tr_app.pdf; and OFAC's *List of Authorized Providers of Air, Travel and Remittance Forwarding Services to Cuba*, revised June 28, 2013, is available at http://www.treasury.gov/resource-center/sanctions/Programs/Documents/cuba_tsp.pdf.

[31] According to a 2007 Government Accountability Office (GAO) report, there are no reliable estimates of total U.S. travel to Cuba because U.S. and Cuban government data are incomplete and cover different populations. See U.S. GAO, Economic Sanctions: Agencies Face Competing Priorities in Enforcing the U.S. Embargo on Cuba, GAO-08-80, November 30, 2007, pp. 31-33. Nevertheless, in May 2004, the inter-agency Commission for Assistance to a Free Cuba estimated that some 160,000-200,000 legal and illegal travelers visited Cuba from the United States annually over the past decade. The Commission maintained that the largest category of legal travel to Cuba consisted of Cuban Americans visiting their families, accounting for 125,000 out of 160,000 total U.S. visitors to Cuba in 2003. See Commission for Assistance to Free Cuba, Report to the President, May 2004, pp. 28 and 36. A July 2007 U.S. International Trade Commission (ITC) report estimated that about 171,000 Americans traveled to Cuba in 2005, and concluded that lifting travel restrictions would result in U.S. travel increasing to between 550,000 and 1 million. U.S. ITC, *U.S. Agricultural Sales to Cuba: Certain Economic Effects of U.S. Restrictions*, USITC Publication 3932, July 2007, pp. xi and 3-14 to 3-17.

[32] Air carrier statistics are derived from a "TranStats" database maintained by the U.S. Department of Transportation, Research and Innovative Technology Administration, Bureau of Transportation Statistics, available at http://www.transtats.bts.gov/homepage.asp.

---

statistics, however, do not reflect Americans that travel to Cuba through other countries, such as Canada, Mexico, or other Latin American and Caribbean nations.

Various press estimates maintain that the overall number of Americans traveling to Cuba in 2011 was some 400,000, with the majority consisting of Cuban Americans visiting family. That number reportedly rose to some 450,000 in 2012, again with the majority consisting of Cuban Americans visiting family.[33]

The Cuban government publishes statistics on travelers to Cuba from the United States, not including Cuban Americans who are excluded from such statistics since Cuba considers them nationals. According to Cuba's statistics, there were just over 98,000 visitors from the United States in 2012, compared to almost 74,000 in 2011 and 63,000 in 2010.[34]

The Florida-based Havana Consulting Group LLC, a business consultancy, reports significantly higher amounts of total U.S. travelers to Cuba. The group cites the same Cuban government statistics noted above to account for non-Cuban American visitors from the United States. However, it also cites a much higher number of Cuban Americans traveling to Cuba than generally cited in the press. For example, the consultancy estimated that a total of almost 574,000 people traveled to Cuban from the United States in 2012, including just over 98,000 in non-Cuban Americans and almost 476,000 Cuban Americans.[35] The group maintains that in 2013, through December 15, the total number of visitors from the United States was just over 569,000, with almost 472,000 Cuban Americans.[36]

General License Categories

- **Family Visits.** Persons subject to the jurisdiction of the United States and persons traveling with them who share a common dwelling as a family visiting a close relative who is a national of Cuba or who is a U.S. government employee assigned to the U.S. Interests Section in Havana without limits on the duration or frequency of visits (31 CFR 515.561(a)). A close relative is defined as any individual related to the traveler by blood, marriage, or adoption who is no more than three generations removed from the traveler or from a common ancestor with the traveler (31 CFR 515.339).

- **Official Government Business.** Officials of the U.S. government, foreign governments, and certain intergovernmental organizations traveling on official business (31 CFR 515.562).

---

[33] For example, see Nick Miroff, "U.S. Trade to Cuba Grows as Restrictions Are Eased," *NPR, All Things Considered,* February 6, 2012; David Harrison, "Cuban Refugees Shouldn't Return, Lawmaker Says," *CQ Today,* May 31, 2012; Marc Frank, "U.S. Congressional Delegation Leave Cuba Empty-Handed," *Reuters News,* February 20, 2013; and Marc Frank, "Americans Traveling to Cuba in Record Numbers," *Reuters News,* October 18, 2013.

[34] Oficina Nacional de Estadísticas (ONE), República de Cuba, "Anuario Estadístico de Cuba, 2012" Edición 2013;

[35] Emilio Morales and Joseph L. Scarpaci, "Miami Leads in Sending Flights to Cuba," The Havana Consulting Group LLC, July 24, 2013.

[36] Emilio Morales, "Año 2013: Record de Remesas y Viajeros a Cuba," The Havana Consulting Group, LLC, December 20, 2013.

- **Journalistic Activity.** Persons regularly employed as journalists by a news reporting organization or by persons regularly employed as supporting broadcast or technical personnel (31 CFR 515.563(a)).

- **Professional Research and Meetings.** Full-time professionals conducting professional research in their areas (provided that the research is of a noncommercial, academic nature; that the research comprises a full work schedule in Cuba; and that the research has a substantial likelihood of public dissemination) or attending professional meetings or conferences in Cuba organized by an international professional organization, institution, or association that regularly sponsors meetings or conferences in other countries (31 CFR 515.564(a)(1) and 515.564(a)(2)). A new category for professional meetings for commercial telecommunications transactions was added in September 2009 (31 CFR 515.564(a)(3)).

- **Educational Activities.** Accredited U.S. graduate and undergraduate degree-making institutions, including faculty, staff, and students involved in (1) participation in a structured educational program in Cuba as part of a course offered for credit by the sponsoring U.S. academic institution; (2) noncommercial academic research in Cuba specifically related to Cuba for the purpose of obtaining a graduate degree; (3) participation in a formal course of study at a Cuban academic institution, provided the formal course of study in Cuba will be accepted for credit toward the student's graduate or undergraduate degree; (4) teaching at a Cuban academic institution by an individual regularly employed in a teaching capacity at the sponsoring U.S. academic institution, provided that the teaching activities are related to an academic program at the Cuban institution and that the duration of the teaching will be no short than 10 weeks; or (5) sponsorship of a Cuban scholar to teach or engage in other scholarly activity at the sponsoring U.S. academic institution (31 CFR 515.565(a)).

- **Religious Activities.** Religious organizations located in the United States, including members and staff of such organizations engaged in a full-time program of religious activities (31 CFR 515.566(a)).

- **Travel Related to Sales of Agricultural Commodities, Medicine, or Medical Devices.** Employees of a producer or distributor of agricultural or medical commodities or an entity representing such a firm. The regulation also sets forth a requirement for written reports, before and after the trip, to be submitted to OFAC describing the purpose and scope of the travel and the business activities conducted (31 CFR 515.533(e)).

- **Travel Related to Sales of Telecommunication Items.** Employees of a U.S. telecommunications services provider or an entity representing such a provider. The regulation also requires written reports to be submitted to OFAC before and after the trip, describing the purpose and scope of the travel and the business activities conducted (31 CFR 515.533(f)).

Specific License Categories

- **Family Visits.** Persons subject to the United States and persons travelling with them who share a common dwelling as a family visiting a close relative who is neither a national of Cuba nor a U.S. government employee assigned to the U.S. Interests Section in Havana. (31 CFR 515.561(b)).

- **Free-lance Journalists.** Travel directly incident to journalistic activities for a free-lance project upon submission of an adequate written application with required documentation (31 CFR 515.563(b)).

- **Professional research and professional meetings.** Travel directly incident to professional research and professional meetings that do not qualify for a general license (31 CFR 515.564(b)).

- **Academic Educational Activities.** Travel for individuals to engage in academic educational activities (noncommercial academic research; participation in a formal course of study at a Cuban academic institution; or teaching at a Cuban academic institution) that are not authorized by a general license for educational activities (31 CFR 515.565(b)(1)).

- **People-to People Exchanges.** Travel for organizations authorizing educational exchanges not involving academic study pursuant to a degree program when those exchanges take place under the auspices of an organization that sponsors and organizes such programs to promote people-to-people contact (31 CFR 515.565(b)(2)).

- **Academic Seminars, Conference, and Workshops.** Accredited U.S. graduate or undergraduate degree-granting academic institutions to sponsor or co-sponsor academic seminars, conference, and workshops related to Cuba or global issues involving Cuba, including attendance at such events by faculty, staff, and students of the licensed institution (31 CFR 515.565(b)(3)).

- **Religious Activities.** Travel for religious activities by individuals or organizations that do not qualify for a general license (31 CFR 515.566(b)).

- **Public Performances, Clinics, Workshops, Athletic and Other Competitions and Exhibitions.** Travel for organizations and individuals participating in a public performance, clinic, workshop, athletic or other competition, or exhibition in Cuba. The event must be open for attendance and, in relevant situations, participation by the Cuban public. All U.S. profits after costs must be donated to an independent nongovernmental organization in Cuba or a U.S.-based charity with the objective, to the extent possible, of promoting people-to-people contact or otherwise benefiting the Cuban people. Such donations are not required for certain amateur or semi-professional athletic competitions held under the auspices of international sports federations. (31 CFR 515.567).

- **Support for the Cuban People.** Those traveling for activities in support of the Cuban people, such as activities of recognized human rights organizations, activities designed to promote a rapid, peaceful transition to democracy, and activities intended to strengthen civil society (31 CFR 515.574).

- **Humanitarian Projects.** Those involved in humanitarian projects in Cuba, such as medical and health-related projects, construction projects, intended to benefit legitimately independent civil society groups, environmental projects, projects involving non-formal educational training, within Cuba or off island, on topics including civil education, journalism, advocacy and organizing, adult literacy and vocational skills, community-based grass roots projects, projects suitable to the development of small-scale enterprise, projects related to agricultural and rural development that promote independent activity, and projects involving the donation of goods to meet basic human needs (31 CFR 515.575).

- **Activities of Private Foundations or Research or Educational Institutes.** Those involved in activities of private foundations or research or education institutes that have an established interest in international relations to collect information related to Cuba for noncommercial purposes (31 CFR 515.576).

- **Exportation, Importation, or Transmission of Information or Informational Materials.** Those involved in the importation, exportation, or transmission of informational materials, defined as publications, films posters, phonograph records, photographs, microfilms, microfiche, tapes, compact disks, CD ROMS, artworks, news wire feeds, and other informational and informational articles (31CFR 515.545(b)).

- **Exportation of Licensable Products**. Those involved in activities related to marketing, sales negotiation, accompanied delivery, or servicing of exports to Cuba authorized by the Department of Commerce and who are not already authorized under general licenses for activities related to marketing and sales of agricultural and medical products or telecommunications services (31CFR 515.533(g)).

Current Restrictions on Remittances

According to a 2007 Government Accountability Office (GAO) report, no reliable data exist for cash remitted directly or indirectly from the United States to Cuba, although the report maintained that data from several sources showed that worldwide remittances to Cuba amounted to between $900 million and $1 billion.[37] More recently in 2013, the State Department reported that remittances were estimated to be between $1.4-$2 billion a year.[38]

Another estimate by the Havana Consulting Group LLC reports significantly higher amounts of cash remittances that have increased from $1.3 billion in 2007 to $2.6 billion in 2012. The group argues that remittances to Cuba have been boosted significantly by several factors, including the Obama Administration's lifting of restrictions on family travel and remittances, economic policy changes in Cuba (such allowing more private sector activities), and reduced wire-transfer costs.[39] For 2013, the Havana Consulting Group maintains that remittances to Cuba grew further to $2.77 billion in 2013, an increase of almost 7%.[40]

U.S. restrictions on such remittances are regulated by the Cuban Assets Control Regulations (CACR) and, just like restrictions on travel, have changed over time.

- **Family Remittances.** As noted above, President Obama announced in April 2009 that restrictions on remittances to family members in Cuba would be lifted. In September 2009, OFAC issued amendments to the CACR implementing the Administration policy changes on remittances. The current regulations authorize a general license for family remittances and remove the limitation on the amount and frequency of family remittances that persons 18 years of age or older may provide to close relatives in Cuba (31 CFR 515.570(a)). As with the travel-related transactions, a close relative is defined as any individual related to the remitter by blood, marriage, or adoption who is no more than three generations removed from the remitter or from a common ancestor with the remitter. The regulations still prohibit remittances to certain officials of the Cuban government and Cuban Communist party. The regulations also authorize two one-time $1,000 emigration-related remittances (31 CFR 515.570(e)), raised from $500 previously. Depository institutions no longer need a specific license for sending remittances to Cuba, although both depository institutions and other licensed remittance forwarders are required to collect information showing compliance with remittance provisions (31 CFR 515.572(a)(3)).

- **Non-Family Remittances.** In January 2011, the Obama Administration restored a general license category for any U.S. person to send remittances of up to $500 per quarter to non-family members in Cuba, including, but not limited to, remittances to support the development of private businesses. These remittances, however, cannot be provided to

---

[37] U.S. Government Accountability Office, *Economic Sanctions: Agencies Face Competing Priorities in Enforcing the U.S. Embargo on Cuba,* GAO-08-80, November 30, 2007, p. 34. In 2004, the Commission for Assistance to a Free Cuba estimated that U.S. cash remittances to Cuba amounted to an estimated $400 million-$800 million per year, although the report also noted that some estimates were as high as $1 billion annually. See Commission for Assistance to a Free Cuba, Report to the President, May 2004, p. 34.

[38] U.S. Department of States, "U.S. Relations with Cuba," Fact Sheet, August 30, 2013.

[39] Emilio Morales and Joseph L. Scarpaci, "Remittances Drive the Cuban Economy," June 11, 2013, and "Opening Up on Both Shorelines Helps Increase Remittances Sent to Cuba in 2011 by About 20%," March 12, 2012, The Havana Consulting Group LLC.

[40] Emilio Morales, "Año 2013: Record de Remesas y Viajeros a Cuba," The Havana Consulting Group, LLC, December 20, 2013.

senior Cuban government officials or senior members of the Cuban Communist Party (31 CFR 515.570(b)).

- **Remittances to Religious Organizations.** In January 2011, the Administration created a general license for remittances to religious institutions in Cuba in support of religious activities (31 CFR 515.570(c)). Prior to this, such remittances were authorized by a specific license.

- **Remittances to U.S. Students in Cuba.** In January 2011, the Administration created a general license authorizing remittances to close relatives who are students in Cuba pursuant to a general or specific license authorizing certain educational activities (31 CFR 515.570(d)).

- **Remittances to Independent Non-governmental Entities and Individuals in Cuba.** Any person subject to U.S. jurisdiction may apply for a specific license to provide remittances to independent non-governmental entities in Cuba, including but not limited to pro-democracy groups and civil society groups, or members of such entities, or to individuals or independent non-governmental entities to support the development of private businesses, including small farms. The types of activities for which transfers will be considered include, but are not limited to, assistance for an independent farmers' cooperative in purchasing goods or support to an independent group in operating a nursing home for the elderly (31 CFR 515.570(g)(1)).

- **Carrying of Remittances to Cuba.** The amount of total authorized remittances that may be carried to Cuba (for all types of remittances) is $3,000 (31 CFR 515.560(c)(4)(i)).

Enforcement of Travel Restrictions: Civil Penalties

Beginning in April 2003, OFAC began making available a regular listing of civil penalties enforcement information for its sanctions programs, including violations of the Cuba travel regulations.[41] According to a Treasury Department spokesman, the information was being made available to make the process more transparent to the public. Under the Trading with the Enemy Act, the Secretary of the Treasury may impose civil fines up to $65,000 per violation of the Cuban Assets Control Regulations.[42] According to OFAC, typical individual penalties have been much lower. Penalties against companies are generally much larger.

Since April 2003, enforcement actions for the Cuba travel regulations have included penalties against the following companies: Metso Minerals, Zim American Israeli Shipping Company, Playboy Enterprises, Omega World Travel, Mr. Travel, Havanatur & Travel Service, American Airlines, Cuba Paquetes, MRP Group Inc., Air Jamaica, Trek Tours (Rhode Island), Premiere Travel of Ohio, Hialeah Gardens Immigration Agency, Only Believe Ministries (Ohio), the

---

[41] See OFAC's website for information on civil enforcement, available at http://www.treasury.gov/resource-center/sanctions/CivPen/Pages/civpen-index2.aspx.

[42] U.S. Department of the Treasury, Office of Foreign Assets Control, "Economic Sanctions Enforcement Guidelines," 74 *Federal Register* 57593-57608, November 9, 2009.

Salvation Army (Texas Division), Beau Rivage Resorts Inc. (Mississippi), E & J Gallo Winery (California), the Four Oaks Foundation (New York), Pioneer Valley Travel (Massachusetts), the International Bicycle Fund (Washington State), Augsburg College (Minnesota), the U.S./Cuba Labor Exchange (Michigan), Coda International Tours Inc. (Florida), Travelocity.com (Texas), American Express Company (Mexico), Lakes Community Credit Union (Michigan), Sonida International (New York), Journey Corporation Travel Management (New York), RMO Inc. (Colorado), Tours International America (California), Aerovacations Inc. (California), Agoda Company (Thailand), Center for Cross Cultural Study Inc. (Massachusetts), Priceline.com (Connecticut), Magic USA Tours (Florida), Philips Electronics of North America Corporation (New York), First Incentive Travel (Florida), American Express Travel Related Services Company (New York), and World Fuel Services Corporation (Florida). Many other companies have received penalties for violating other aspects of the Cuba embargo regulations, including some that have been assessed multi-million dollar penalties.[43]

In July 2013, American Express Travel Related Services Inc. (TRS) agreed to pay $5.2 million for violations of the travel regulations from December 2005 to November 2011 when it issued more than 14,000 tickets for travel between Cuba and countries other than the United States. OFAC maintained that TRS expressed "reckless disregard for the CACR" because of similar apparent violations in 1995 and 1996, the lack of oversight by its U.S. management of TRS' foreign offices, and the failure to implement effective mechanisms for detecting Cuba travel bookings until late 2010 after having informed OFAC in 1995 and 1996 that it would do so.[44] Cuba's Ministry of Foreign Affairs criticized the action as reflecting the "U.S. obsession of preventing American citizens from freely traveling to Cuba, at all costs."[45]

In addition to civil penalties against companies, OFAC has also sanctioned individuals for violating the travel sanctions. According to OFAC's listing of civil enforcement actions on its website, from 2004-2005, over 800 individuals had civil penalties assessed or reached informal settlements for alleged violations of various restrictions under the Cuban Assets Control Regulations. The individuals either were assessed a penalty or reached an informal settlement for violations of the Cuba regulations (not just travel-related restrictions) with almost $1.1 million in penalties. Since 2006, however, after backlogged cases were resolved, the number of individuals penalized by OFAC fell considerably. Less than 100 individuals have been penalized since 2006, with 21 in 2006, 17 in 2007, 32 in 2008, 3 in 2009, and 1 in 2010; since 2011, OFAC has not reported any individuals being penalized for violations of the CACR.

Arguments for Lifting Cuba Travel Restrictions

Those who argue in favor of lifting restrictions on travel to Cuba contend that the travel ban hinders U.S. efforts to influence political and economic conditions in Cuba. They maintain that the best way to realize change in Cuba is to lift restrictions, allowing a flood of U.S. citizens to travel and engage in conversations with average Cubans. They point to the influence of person-to-

---

[43] For example, ING Bank, N.V. of the Netherlands reached a $619 million settlement with OFAC in June 2012 for violating U.S. sanction regimes against Cuba, Iran, Burma, Sudan and Libya. The Cuban sanctions violations accounted for the majority of the bank's settlement. See: U.S. Department of the Treasury, Office of Foreign Assets Control, "Enforcement Information for June 12, 2012."

[44] U.S. Department of the Treasury, Office of Foreign Assets Control, "Enforcement Information for July 22, 2013."

[45] "Cuba Denounces Reinforcement of U.S. Blockade," *BBC Monitoring Americas*, July 31, 2013.

person contact in Russia and Eastern European nations, which they argue ultimately helped lead to the fall of communism in the Soviet bloc. They maintain that restricting travel by ordinary Americans prevents interaction and information exchanges with ordinary Cubans, exchanges that can help break down the Cuban government's tight control and manipulation of news; that the current travel ban actually supports the Cuban government in its efforts to restrict information provided to the Cuban people; and that it in effect supports the Cuban government's totalitarian control over the Cuban nation.

A second argument made by those who want to lift travel restrictions is that the ban abridges the rights of ordinary Americans to travel. They contend that such restrictions on the right to travel subvert the first amendment right of free speech. They maintain that the U.S. government should not limit the categories of travelers who can visit Cuba or subject many prospective travelers to the requirement of applying for specific licenses, subject to denial, in order to engage in people-to-people contact.

Those in favor of lifting the travel ban also argue that U.S. citizens can travel to other communist or authoritarian governments around the world, such as the People's Republic of China, Vietnam, Burma, and Iran. They point out that Americans could travel to the Soviet Union before its breakup. Supporters of changing travel policy toward Cuba argue that their proposals would still allow the President to prohibit such travel in times of war or armed hostilities, or if there were imminent danger to the health or safety of Americans. They argue that these conditions do not exist with regard to Cuba, and point to a May 1998 Defense Intelligence Agency report that concluded that "Cuba does not pose a significant military threat to the U.S. or to other countries in the region."[46]

Supporters of lifting the travel restrictions maintain that such a move could be done without lifting the underlying U.S. embargo on trade and financial transactions with Cuba. They point to the 1977-1982 period when the travel ban was essentially lifted, but the overall embargo remained in place.

Finally, some supporters of lifting the travel restrictions argue that the U.S. economy would benefit from increased demand for air and cruise travel, which reportedly would expand U.S. economic output, and from increased U.S. agricultural exports to Cuba. According to a 2002 report prepared for the Center for International Policy, a policy group that advocates lifting the embargo, U.S. economic output would expand by $1.18 billion-$1.61 billion, with the creation of between 16,888 and 23,020 jobs if travel restrictions were lifted.[47] The U.S. International Trade Commission (USITC) produced a study in 2007 (updated in 2009), examining the effects of lifting U.S. restrictions on travel to Cuba and restrictions on U.S. government financing for agricultural exports to Cuba on the level of U.S. agricultural sales to Cuba. The USITC 2009 update found that the U.S. share of Cuba's agricultural imports would have increased from 38% to between 49% and 64% absent the financing and travel restrictions.[48]

---

[46] Defense Intelligence Agency. Report on Cuban Threat to U.S. National Security. May 6, 1998.

[47] *The Impact on the U.S. Economy of Lifting Restrictions on Travel to Cuba*, The Brattle Group, Washington, DC. Prepared by Dorothy Robyn, James D. Reitzes, and Bryan Church. July 15, 2002.

[48] USITC, *U.S. Agricultural Sales to Cuba: Certain Economic Effects of U.S. Restrictions,* USITC Publication 3932, July 2007, available at http://www.usitc.gov/publications/332/pub3932.pdf; USITC, *U.S. Agricultural Sales to Cuba: Certain Economic Effects of U.S. Restrictions, An Update,* Office of Industries Working Paper, by Jonathan R. Coleman, No. ID-22, June 2009, available at http://www.usitc.gov/publications/332/working_papers/ID-22.pdf.

Arguments for Maintaining Cuba Travel Restrictions

Those favoring the continuation of restrictions on travel to Cuba point out that there are already significant provisions in U.S. law permitting Americans to travel there for legitimate reasons that support the Cuban people and not the Cuban government. They point out that thousands of Americans travel to Cuba legally under the various provisions of the Cuban embargo regulations, and that now Cuban Americans may visit close relatives without restrictions. Other categories of travel allowed include students, journalists, researchers, artists, musicians, and athletes.

A second argument made for maintaining restrictions on travel to Cuba is that lifting the travel ban entirely will open the floodgates to American tourist travel that will support Raúl Castro's rule by providing his government with millions in tourist receipts. Advocates of restricting travel oppose any loosening that could prolong the Castro regime by propping it up with increased income. In contrast to those supporting tourist travel, they believe that continued travel restrictions will help influence Cuba's policy. They argue that since the collapse of the Soviet Union and the loss of Soviet subsidies to Cuba, the travel and embargo regulations have contributed to the Cuban government's decision to cut the military's size and budget by half since 1989 and to introduce limited economic reforms. Lifting travel restrictions, they argue, would eliminate the U.S. leverage on Cuba to enact further reforms and to improve the human rights situation.

Those favoring the maintenance of travel restrictions argue that the reality of the human rights situation dispels the notion that American tourists would be engaging in exchanges with ordinary Cubans. They maintain that the thousands of European, Canadian, and other tourists who travel to Cuba each year largely stay in tourist hotels have no discernible effect on the human rights situation in Cuba.

Some opposed to lifting travel restrictions argue that there should not be tourist travel as long as Cuba provides refuge to violent criminals who have escaped U.S. justice. While the current number of U.S. fugitives from justice is uncertain, the State Department, in its *Country Reports on Terrorism 2007*, stated that there were more than 70 fugitives from U.S. justice living in Cuba, including convicted murderers and hijackers, most of whom entered Cuba in the 1970s.

Finally, many opponents of legislation to lift the Cuba travel restrictions argue that the authority to impose such restrictions is an important foreign policy tool for the President. They point out that the President has the authority to restrict travel when it is in the national security or foreign policy interests of the United States, and has utilized that policy tool when needed. They point to past instances of restricting travel to Libya, Vietnam, and North Korea. With regard to Cuba, they point to the 1984 Supreme Court decision in the case of *Regan v. Wald* that upheld restrictions on travel to Cuba imposed by the Reagan Administration.

Legislative Initiatives in the 113th Congress

As reported by the Appropriations Committees in July 2013, the House and Senate versions of the FY2014 Financial Services and General Government appropriations measure, H.R. 2786 and S. 1371, had different provisions regarding U.S. policy regarding travel to Cuba. The House version would have tightened restrictions on travel by prohibiting funding for any additional authorization of people-to-people exchanges during the fiscal year, while the Senate version would have eased restrictions on travel by authorizing a new general license for professional travel related to disaster prevention, emergency preparedness, and natural resource protection. Ultimately, however, none of these provision were included in the FY2014 omnibus appropriations measure, H.R. 3547 (P.L. 113-76), signed into law January 17, 2014.

As reported out of the House Appropriations committee on July 23, 2013, H.R. 2786 (H.Rept. 113-172) had a provision in Section 124 that would have prohibited FY2014 funding used "to approve, license, facilitate, authorize, or otherwise allow" travel-related or other transactions related to nonacademic educational exchanges (i.e. people-to-people travel) to Cuba set forth in 31 CFR 515.565(b)(2) of the CACR. The committee report to the House bill contended that this category of travel violates the prohibition on travel related to tourist activities set forth in the Trade Sanctions Reform and Export Enhancement Act of 2000 (P.L. 106-387, Title IX). The report also maintained that the stated purpose of people-to-people travel – to promote the Cuban people's independence from Cuban authorities – "cannot be accomplished through itineraries that mainly feature interactions with representatives of a dictatorship that actively oppresses the Cuban people, nor can it be accomplished through itineraries that do not require meetings with pro-democracy activists or independent members of Cuban civil society."

The House bill had a second Cuba provision in Section 125 that would have require a Treasury Department report within 90 days of the bill's enactment with information for each fiscal year since FY2007 on the number of travelers visiting close relatives in Cuba; the average duration of these trips; the average amount of U.S. dollars spent per family traveler (including amount of remittances carried to Cuba); the number of return trips per year; and the total sum of U.S. dollars spent collectively by family travelers for each fiscal year.

As reported out of the Senate Appropriations Committee on July 25, 2013, S. 1371 (S.Rept. 113-80) had a provision in Section 628 that would have provided for a new general license for travel-related transactions for full-time professional research; attendance at professional meetings if the sponsoring organization is a U.S. organization; and the organization and management of professional meetings and conferences in Cuba if the sponsoring organization is a U.S. professional organization – *if* the travel is related to disaster prevention, emergency preparedness, and natural resource protection, including for fisheries, coral reefs, and migratory species. This provision would have expanded the current general licenses available for professional research and meetings in Cuba that allow full-time professionals to conduct professional research in their areas (with certain conditions), attend professional meetings or conferences in Cuba organized by an international professional organization, and attend professional meetings for commercial telecommunications transactions (31 CFR 515.564).

Several other initiatives again have been introduced that would lift all travel restrictions: H.R. 871 (Rangel) would lift travel restrictions; H.R. 873 (Rangel) would lift travel restrictions and restrictions on U.S. agricultural exports; and H.R. 214 (Serrano), H.R. 872 (Rangel), and H.R. 1917 (Rush) would lift the overall embargo, including travel restrictions.

Appendix. Legislative Action from the 106th to the 112th Congress

Legislative Initiatives in the 112th Congress

As noted above, there were several attempts in the first session of the 112th Congress aimed at rolling back the Obama Administration's actions easing restrictions on travel and remittances, but none of these were approved. Several legislative initiatives were also introduced that would have further eased or lifted such restrictions altogether, but no action was taken on these measures.

FAA Reauthorization

During consideration of the Federal Aviation Administration reauthorization bill, S. 223, in February 2011, an amendment was submitted, but never considered, **S.Amdt. 61** (Rubio), that would have prohibited an expansion of flights to locations in countries that are state sponsors of terrorism (which includes Cuba).

FY2012 Financial Services and General Government Appropriations

The House Appropriations Committee reported its version of the FY2012 Financial Services and General Government Appropriations bill, **H.R. 2434**, on July 7, 2011, with a provision in Section 901 that would have rolled back the Obama Administration's actions easing restrictions on family travel and on remittances overall. (The Senate Appropriations Committee version of the measure, **S. 1573**, did not contain a similar provision.) The House provision had been offered as an amendment by Representative Mario Diaz-Balart that was agreed to by voice vote during the committee's June 24, 2011, markup of the measure. The provision would have repealed amendments to the Cuban Assets Control Regulations made since January 19, 2009, regarding family travel (31 CFR 515.561), carrying remittances (31 CFR 515.560(c)(4)(i)), and sending remittances to Cuba (31 CFR 515.570). According to the provision, such regulations would be restored and carried out as in effect on January 19, 2009, notwithstanding any guidelines, opinions, letters, presidential directives, or agency practices relating to such regulations that are issued or carried out after such date.

If the provision were to be enacted, family travel would be limited to once every three years for a period of up to 14 days and would require a specific license from the Treasury Department; licensed travelers would be allowed to carry just $300 in remittances compared to the $3,000 currently allowed; family remittances would be limited to $300 per quarter; non-family remittances restored by the Obama Administration, up to $500 per quarter, would not be allowed; and the general license for remittances to religious organizations would be eliminated, with such remittances permitted via specific license.

The White House's Statement of Administration Policy on H.R. 2434, issued July 13, 2011, stated that Administration opposed Section 901 because it would reverse the President's policy on family travel and remittances, and that the President's senior advisors would recommend a veto if the bill contained the provision. According to the statement, Section 901 "would undo the President's efforts to increase contact between divided Cuban families, undermine the enhancement of the Cuban people's economic independence and support for private sector activity in Cuba that come from increased remittances from family members, and therefore isolate the Cuban people and make them more dependent on Cuban authorities."[49]

A second Cuba amendment agreed to by voice vote during the markup of H.R. 2434 was offered by Representative Jeff Flake. The amendment made changes to the committee report to the bill (H.Rept. 112-136) and would have required a report from OFAC on the current number of pending applications seeking specific licenses related to educational exchanges not involving academic study pursuant to a degree program under the auspices of an organization that sponsors and organizes such programs to promote people-to-people contact. The report also would have required information on the number of these licenses that OFAC has approved to date, its plan for getting through the current queue of license applications, and its plan for expeditiously reviewing those applications in the future.

In November 2011, an attempt to include the Senate version of the Financial Services appropriations measure, S. 1573, in a "minibus" with two other full-year appropriations measures and a short-term continuing resolution failed in part because of disagreement over a Cuba provision that would have allowed direct transfers from a Cuban financial institution to a U.S. financial institution to pay for U.S. agricultural and medical exports to Cuba. (For background on that provision see CRS Report R41617, *Cuba: Issues for the 112th Congress* and CRS Report R42008, *Financial Services and General Government: FY2012 Appropriations*.)

In December 2011, a legislative battle ensued over the Consolidated Appropriations Act, FY2012, **H.R. 2055**, a "megabus" bill that combined nine full-year appropriations measures, including the Financial Services and General Government bill. At issue was the potential inclusion of two Cuba provisions that had been in the House Appropriations Committee-approved version of the Financial Services bill, H.R. 2434: one described above that would roll back to January 2009 the Obama Administration's actions easing restrictions on family travel and on remittances; and the second a provision that would continue to clarify, for the third fiscal year in a row, the definition of "payment of cash in advance" for U.S. agricultural and medical exports to Cuba so that the payment was due upon delivery in Cuba as opposed to being due before the goods left U.S. ports. (The text of the two Cuba provisions was also included in Division C, Sections 632 and 634, of **H.R. 3671**, a new "megabus" bill introduced by House Republicans on December 14, 2011.)

Ultimately congressional leaders agreed to not include the two Cuba provisions in H.R. 2055 (H.Rept. 112-331) and the measure was approved by the House and Senate, respectively, on December 16 and 17, 2011, and signed into law on December 23, 2011 (P.L. 112-74). The White House reportedly had exerted strong pressure not to include the Cuba provision that would have rolled back the Administration's easing of restrictions on travel and remittances. Dropping the second provision on the definition of "payment of cash in advance" for U.S. agricultural and medical products appears to have been a political tradeoff made to compensate for the travel rollback provision being dropped.

FY2012 Foreign Relations Authorization Act

In other congressional action, on July 21, 2011, the House Committee on Foreign Affairs marked up **H.R. 2583** (H.Rept. 112-223), the FY2012 Foreign Relations Authorization Act, with a

---

[49] Executive Office of the President, Office of Management and Budget, Statement of Administration Policy, H.R. 2434 – Financial Services and General Government Appropriations Act, 2012, July 13, 2011.

provision (§1126 of the reported bill) that would have required the President to fully enforce all U.S. regulations on travel to Cuba as in effect on January 19, 2009, and impose the corresponding penalties against individuals determined to be in violation of such regulations. The provision was added by an amendment offered by Representative David Rivera, approved 36-6, that had the intent of reinstating tighter travel restrictions as they existed under the Bush Administration in January 2009.

Amendments to the Cuban Adjustment Act

Two additional measures introduced in August 2011 would have amended the Cuban Adjustment Act of 1966 (CAA, P.L. 89-732) in order to curb travel to Cuba by Cubans who had recently immigrated to the United States. Introduced on August 1, 2011, **H.R. 2771** (Rivera) would have amended the CAA to increase to five years the period during which a Cuban national must be physically present in the United States in order to qualify for adjustment of status to that of a permanent resident. The legislation also would have provided that an alien would be ineligible for adjustment to permanent resident status if the alien returned to Cuba after admission or parole into the United States before becoming a U.S. citizen. A subsequent version, H.R. 2831 (Rivera), introduced August 30, 2011, just contained the provision maintaining that an alien from Cuba would be ineligible for adjustment to permanent resident status under the CAA if he or she returned to Cuba before becoming a U.S. citizen. The House Committee on the Judiciary, Subcommittee on Immigration on Policy Enforcement, held a hearing on H.R. 2831 on May 31, 2012 (available at http://judiciary.house.gov/hearings/Hearings%202012/hear_05312012_3.html).

Initiatives to Ease Restrictions on Travel and Remittances

In contrast to measures aimed at rolling back the Obama Administration's polices easing travel and remittances to Cuba, several measures would have eased or lifted travel restrictions altogether. **H.R. 1886** (Rangel) would have prohibited restrictions on travel to Cuba. **H.R. 1888** (Rangel), in addition to removing some restrictions on the export of U.S. agricultural products to Cuba, would also have prohibited Cuba travel restrictions. Two initiatives that would have lifted the overall embargo on trade and restrictions on financial transaction with Cuba, **H.R. 255** (Serrano) and **H.R. 1887** (Rangel), would also have lifted restrictions on travel and remittances to Cuba. **H.R. 380** (Lee) would have provided that no funds made available to the Department of the Treasury could be used to implement, administer, or enforce regulations to require specific licenses for travel-related transactions directly related to educational activities in Cuba.

Legislative Initiatives in the 111th Congress

The 111th Congress took action in March 2009 to ease restrictions on family travel and travel for the marketing and sale of agricultural and medical goods. The eased family travel restrictions were superseded by the Obama Administration's April 2009 action to allow unlimited family travel and remittances. At the same time, the Administration also eased restrictions for travel for telecommunications-related sales and for attendance at professional meetings related to commercial telecommunications. Numerous other bills introduced in the 111th Congress would have lifted or eased restrictions on travel and remittances to Cuba, but these restrictions were not considered. One House initiative, H.R. 4645 (Peterson), would have lifted all restrictions on travel to Cuba and also would have eased restrictions on the payment mechanisms for U.S. agricultural exports to Cuba. The House Agriculture Committee approved the measure, but no further action was taken on the bill.

First Session Action

On March 11, 2009, President Obama signed into law the Omnibus Appropriations Act, 2009 (P.L. 111-8), with two provisions easing restrictions on travel to Cuba. (The provisions were identical to provisions that had been included in the Senate Appropriations Committee version of the FY2009 Financial Services and General Government Appropriations bill in the 110th Congress, S. 3260.)

In the enacted bill, Section 620 of Division D, Financial Services and General Government Appropriations Act, 2009, amended the Trade Sanctions Reform and Export Enhancement Act of 2000 (TSRA) to require the Secretary of the Treasury to issue regulations for travel to, from, or within Cuba under a general license for the marketing and sale of agricultural and medical goods, meaning that there would be no requirement to obtain special permission from OFAC. Such travel had required a specific license from OFAC, issued on a case-by-case basis. OFAC issued regulations implementing this provision on September 3, 2009.

Section 621 of Division D prohibited funds from being used to administer, implement, or enforce family travel restrictions that were imposed by the Bush Administration in June 2004. OFAC implemented this provision by reinstating a general license for family travel as it existed prior to the Bush Administration's tightening of restrictions in June 2004. As implemented by the Treasury Department, travel was allowed once every 12 months to visit a close relative for an unlimited length of stay, and the limit for daily expenditure allowed by family travelers became the same as for other authorized travelers to Cuba (the State Department maximum per diem rate for Havana). The new general license also expanded the definition of "close relative" to mean any individual related to the traveler by blood, marriage, or adoption who is no more than three generations removed from that person. This provision was superseded by the Obama Administration's further liberalization of family travel to Cuba announced in April 2009.

The joint explanatory statement to P.L. 111-8 also required the Department of the Treasury to prepare a report within 90 days on the steps that it is taking to assess OFAC's allocation of resources for investigating and penalizing violations of the Cuba embargo with respect to the numerous other sanctions programs it administers. As part of the report, the Treasury Department was directed to provide detailed information on OFAC's Cuba-related licensing on its enforcement of the Cuba embargo.

On November 19, 2009, the House Committee on Foreign Affairs held a hearing on U.S. restrictions on travel to Cuba entitled "Is it Time to Lift the Ban on Travel to Cuba?" that featured former U.S. government officials and other private witnesses.

Second Session Action

In the second session, the only legislative action related to Cuba travel restrictions occurred in the House Committee on Agriculture, and no subsequent action was taken. On March 11, 2010, the committee held a hearing to review U.S. agricultural sales to Cuba. At the hearing, there was discussion of recently introduced H.R. 4645 (Peterson), a measure that would remove restrictions on travel to Cuba and also remove some restrictions regarding payments for U.S. agricultural exports to Cuba. On June 30, 2010, the committee reported out H.R. 4645 by a vote of 25-20 (H.Rept. 111-653). The bill would have lifted all restrictions on travel to Cuba. It also included two provisions easing restrictions on the payment mechanisms for U.S. agricultural exports to Cuba. The House Committee on Foreign Affairs was scheduled to hold a markup of the bill on

September 29, 2010, but postponed its consideration, and in the aftermath of the 2011 U.S. legislative elections, no further action was taken. An identical companion bill in the Senate, S. 3112 (Klobuchar), was introduced March 15, 2010, and referred to the Committee on Foreign Relations.

On April 29, 2010, the House Ways and Means Committee, Subcommittee on Trade, held a hearing on U.S.-Cuba policy that examined whether relaxing current Cuba travel and trade restrictions would advance U.S. economic objectives, as well as U.S. political and human rights goals in Cuba.

Additional Initiatives in the 111th Congress

Several other legislative initiatives were introduced in the 111th Congress that would have eased restrictions on travel to Cuba, but no action was taken on these measures. H.R. 874 (Delahunt)/S. 428 (Dorgan) and H.R. 1528 (Rangel) would have prohibited restrictions on travel to Cuba. H.R. 188 (Serrano), H.R. 1530 (Rangel), and H.R. 2272 (Rush) would have lifted the overall embargo on trade and financial transactions with Cuba, including travel restrictions. H.R. 1531 (Rangel)/S. 1089 (Baucus) would have facilitated the export of U.S. agricultural products to Cuba and also would have prohibited restrictions on travel to Cuba. H.R. 332 (Lee) would have eased restrictions on educational travel by providing that no funds made available to the Department of the Treasury may be used to implement, administer, or enforce regulations to require specific licenses for travel-related transactions directly related to educational activities in Cuba. S. 774 (Dorgan), H.R. 1918 (Flake), and S. 1517 (Murkowski) would have amended the Trade Sanctions Reform and Economic Enhancement Act of 2000 to require the Secretary of the Treasury to authorize travel to Cuba under a general license in connection to hydrocarbon exploration and extraction activities. In contrast, H.Con.Res. 132 (Tiahrt) would have called for the fulfillment of certain democratic conditions before the United States increases trade and tourism to Cuba.

Legislative Initiatives in the 110th Congress

In the 110th Congress, several House and Senate committee versions of appropriations bills had provisions that would have eased restrictions on travel to Cuba in various ways, but none of these provisions were included in final enacted legislation. Numerous other bills were introduced that would have eased restrictions on travel and remittance in various ways, but no action was taken on these measures.

First Session Action

In the first session of the 110th Congress, two Senate Appropriations Committee-reported versions of appropriations bills had provisions that would have eased restrictions on travel to Cuba for the marketing and sale of agricultural and medical goods, but ultimately these provisions were not included in the FY2008 Consolidated Appropriations Act (P.L. 110-161). The Senate version of the FY2008 Financial Services and General Government appropriations bill, reported July 19, 2007, H.R. 2829, had a provision in Section 620 that would eased such travel restrictions, while the Senate version of the FY2008 Agriculture appropriations bill, S. 1859, reported July 24, 2007, had such a provision in Section 741.

Second Session Action

In the second session, several versions of House and Senate appropriations bills had provisions easing Cuba travel restrictions and other Cuba sanctions, but none of these were included in the FY2009 continuing resolution. The House Appropriations Committee approved its version of the Financial Services and General Government Appropriations bill for FY2009 on June 25, 2008, which contained provisions in Title VI that would have eased restrictions on the sale of U.S. agricultural exports to Cuba and on family travel to Cuba. The committee ultimately introduced and reported the bill, H.R. 7323, on December 10, 2008 (H.Rept. 110-920). With regard to family travel, Section 622 would have allowed for such travel once a year (instead of the current restriction of once every three years), while Section 623 would have expanded such travel by a person to visit an aunt, uncle, niece, nephew, or first cousin (instead of the current restriction limiting such travel to visit a spouse, child, grandchild, parent, grandparent, or sibling).

On July 14, 2008, the Senate Appropriations Committee reported its version of the FY2009 Financial Services and General Government Appropriations bill, S. 3260 (S.Rept. 110-417), which included provisions easing restrictions on family travel and on travel to Cuba relating to the commercial sale of agricultural and medical goods. With regard to family travel, Section 620 would have provided that no funds could be used to administer, implement, or enforce the Administration's June 2004 tightening of restrictions related to travel to visit relatives in Cuba. With regard to travel for agricultural or medical sales, Section 619 would have allowed for a general license for such travel instead of a specific license that requires permission from the Treasury Department.

On July 21, 2008, the Senate Appropriations Committee reported its version of the FY2009 Agriculture Appropriations bill, S. 3289 (S.Rept. 110-426), with a provision in Section 737 that would have eased restrictions on travel to Cuba for the sale of agricultural and medical goods. The provision would have allowed for a general license for such travel instead of a specific license that requires permission from the Treasury Department. The measure had been approved by the committee on July 17, 2008.

Additional Initiatives in the 110th Congress

A number of other initiatives introduced in the 110th Congress would have eased Cuba travel restrictions. H.R. 654 (Rangel), S. 721 (Enzi), and Section 254 of S. 554 (Dorgan) would prohibit the President from regulating or prohibiting travel to Cuba or any of the transactions incident to travel. Two bills that would lift overall economic sanctions—H.R. 217 (Serrano) and H.R. 624 (Rangel)—would also lift travel restrictions. H.R. 177 (Lee) would ease restrictions on educational travel to Cuba. H.R. 757 (Delahunt) would lift restrictions on family travel and the provision of remittances for family members in Cuba. H.R. 1026 (Moran, Jerry), which would facilitate the sale of U.S. agricultural products to Cuba, includes a provision that would provide for general license authority for travel-related transactions for people involved in agricultural sales and marketing activities or in the transportation of such sales. H.R. 2819 (Rangel) and S. 1673 (Baucus), which would ease restrictions on U.S. agricultural and medical exports to Cuba, would also lift restrictions on travel to Cuba. The Senate Committee on Finance held a hearing on S. 1673 on December 11, 2007.

Legislative Initiatives in the Aftermath of 2008 Hurricanes

In the aftermath of the Hurricanes Gustav and Ike that struck Cuba in late August and early September 2008, several legislative initiatives were introduced that would have temporarily eased U.S. embargo restrictions in several areas, including restrictions on family travel, remittances, the provision of gift parcels, and the sale of relief supplies to Cuba. On September 15, 2008, Senator Dodd offered S.Amdt. 5581 to the Department of Defense authorization bill (S. 3001) that would have, for a 180-day period: allowed unrestricted family travel; eased restrictions on remittances by removing the limit and allowing any American to send remittances to Cuba; expanded the list of allowable items that may be included in gift parcels; and allowed for unrestricted U.S. cash sales of food, medicines, and relief supplies to Cuba. The amendment was not considered, and therefore not part of the final bill.

In the House, two legislative initiatives were introduced in the aftermath of the hurricanes that would have temporarily eased restrictions in various ways. On September 16, 2008, Representative Flake introduced H.R. 6913, which would have prohibited any funds from going to the Department of Commerce to implement, administer, or enforce tightened restrictions on the contents of gift parcels to Cuba that were introduced in June 2004. On September 18, 2008, Representative Delahunt introduced H.R. 6962, the Humanitarian Relief to Cuba Act, which would have, for a 180-day period: allowed unrestricted family travel; eased restrictions on remittances by removing the limit and allowing any American to send remittances to Cuba; and expanded the list of allowable items that may be included in gift parcels.

Legislative Initiatives in the 109th Congress

In the 109th Congress, several amendments to FY2006 and FY2007 appropriations bills that would have eased Cuba travel restrictions in various ways and restrictions on sending gift parcels to Cuba were defeated. Several bills were introduced that would have lifted or eased restrictions on travel and the provision of remittances to Cuba, but no action was taken on these measures.

First Session Action

On June 30, 2005, the House rejected three amendments easing Cuba sanctions to H.R. 3058, the FY2006 Transportation, Treasury, Housing and Urban Development, Judiciary, District of Columbia, and Independent Agencies Appropriations Act. The amendments failed during House floor consideration: H.Amdt. 420 (Davis) on family travel, by a vote of 208-211; H.Amdt. 422 (Lee) on educational travel, by a vote of 187-233; and H.Amdt. 424 (Rangel) on the overall embargo, by a vote of 169-250. An additional amendment on religious travel, H.Amdt. 421 (Flake), was withdrawn, and an amendment on family travel by members of the U.S. military, H.Amdt. 419 (Flake), was ruled out of order for constituting legislation in an appropriations bill. The introduction of H.Amdt. 419 was prompted by the case of a U.S. military member who served in Iraq, Sergeant Carlos Lazo, who was prohibited from visiting his two sons in Cuba because he last visited there in 2003.

During June 29, 2005, Senate consideration of H.R. 2361, the FY2006 Interior, Environment, and Related Agencies Appropriations Act, the Senate rejected (60-35; a two-thirds majority vote was required) a motion to suspend the rules with respect to S.Amdt. 1059 (Dorgan), which would have allowed travel to Cuba under a general license for the purpose of visiting a member of the person's immediate family for humanitarian reasons. The amendment was then ruled out of order.

Its introduction had also been prompted by the case of Sergeant Carlos Lazo, who wanted to visit his sons in Cuba, one of whom was gravely sick.

On June 15, 2005, the House rejected (210-216) H.Amdt. 270 (Flake) to H.R. 2862, the FY2006 Science, State, Justice, Commerce, and Related Agencies Appropriations Act. The amendment would have prohibited the use of funds to implement, administer, or enforce June 2004 tightened restrictions on sending gift parcels to Cuba. H.Amdt. 269 (McDermott), which would have prohibited the use of funds in the bill to prosecute any individual for travel to Cuba, was offered but subsequently withdrawn.

During April 6, 2005, Senate floor consideration of the FY2006 and FY2007 Foreign Affairs Authorization Act, S. 600, the Senate considered S.Amdt. 281 (Baucus) and a second-degree amendment, S.Amdt. 282 (Craig) that would have facilitated the sale of U.S. agricultural products to Cuba. The language of the amendments consisted of the provisions of S. 328 (Craig), the Agricultural Export Facilitation Act of 2005, which included a provision for a general license for travel transactions related to the marketing and sale of agricultural products, as opposed to the current requirement of a specific license for such travel transactions. Neither action on the amendments nor on S. 600 was completed.

Second Session Action

On June 14, 2006, the House rejected two amendments to the FY2007 Transportation/Treasury appropriation bill, H.R. 5576 that would have eased Cuba travel restrictions. H.Amdt. 1050 (Rangel), rejected by a vote of 183-245, would have prohibited funds from being used to implement the overall economic embargo of Cuba. H.Amdt. 1051 (Lee), rejected by a vote of 187-236, would have prohibited funds from being used to implement the Administration's June 2004 tightening of restrictions on educational travel to Cuba. An additional Cuba amendment, H.Amdt. 1032 (Flake), would have prohibited the use of funds to amend regulations relating to travel for religious activities in Cuba; it was withdrawn from consideration.

In other action, on June 22, 2006, the Senate Appropriations Committee reported its version of the FY2007 Agriculture appropriations bill, H.R. 5384 (S.Rept. 109-266), which contained a provision (§755) liberalizing travel to Cuba related to the sale of agricultural and medical goods. The provision would have provided for such travel under a general license, instead of under a specific license as currently allowed, issued on a case-by-case basis by the Treasury Department. Final action on the appropriations measure was not completed by the end of the 109th Congress. Similar Senate provisions in FY2004 and FY2005 agricultural appropriations bills were stripped out of the final enacted measures.

Additional Initiatives in the 109th Congress

A number of other legislative initiatives were introduced in the 109th Congress that would have eased restrictions on travel and remittances to Cuba. Two bills—S. 894 (Enzi) and H.R. 1814 (Flake)—would have specifically lifted overall restrictions on travel to Cuba. H.R. 2617 (Davis) would have prohibited any additional restrictions on per diem allowances, family visits to Cuba, remittances, and accompanied baggage beyond those that were in effect on June 15, 2004. H.R. 3064 (Lee) would have prohibited the use of funds available to the Department of the Treasury to implement regulations from June 2004 that tightened restrictions on travel to Cuba for educational activities. H.Con.Res. 206 (Serrano), introduced in the aftermath of Hurricane Dennis that struck Cuba in July 2005 (causing 16 deaths and significant damage), would have expressed the sense of Congress that the President should temporarily suspend restrictions on remittances, gift parcels, and family travel to Cuba to allow Cuban-Americans to assist their relatives.

Two bills—H.R. 208 (Serrano) and H.R. 579 (Paul)—would have lifted the overall embargo on trade and financial transactions with Cuba, including restrictions on travel and remittances to Cuba.

Finally, two identical bills dealing with easing restrictions on exporting agricultural commodities to Cuba—H.R. 719 (Moran of Kansas) and S. 328 (Craig)—included provisions that would have provided for a general license for travel transactions related to the marketing and sale of agricultural products, as opposed to the current requirement of a specific license for such travel transactions.

Legislative Initiatives in the 108th Congress[50]

In the 108th Congress, several FY2004 and FY2005 appropriations bills had provisions that would have eased Cuba travel restrictions in various ways, but ultimately these provisions were not included in final appropriations measures. The Administration had threatened to veto legislation if it contained provisions weakening Cuba sanctions. In addition, several bills in the 108th Congress were introduced that specifically would have lifted or eased restrictions on travel to Cuba, but no action was taken on these measures.

First Session Action

Since action on FY2003 Treasury Department appropriations was not completed before the end of the 107th Congress, the 108th Congress faced early action on it and other unfinished FY2003 appropriations measures. The final version of the FY2003 omnibus appropriations measure, H.J.Res. 2 (P.L. 108-7), which included Treasury Department appropriations, did not include provisions affecting restrictions on travel to Cuba. The White House had threatened to veto the measure if it contained provisions weakening the embargo. While the Senate version did not include the Senate Appropriations Committee provision from the 107th Congress that would have eased travel restrictions by prohibiting any funding for enforcing the Cuba travel regulations, it did include a provision (contained in Division J, Section 124) that would have expedited action on travel applications for travel by OFAC within 90 days of receipt. Ultimately, however, the Senate provision was dropped in the conference report (H.Rept. 108-10) on the omnibus measure.

Both the House and Senate versions of the FY2004 Transportation-Treasury appropriations bill, H.R. 2989, had nearly identical provisions that would have prevented funds from being used to administer or enforce restrictions on travel or travel-related transactions. But the provisions were dropped in the conference report to the FY2004 Consolidated Appropriations Act, P.L. 108-199 (H.R. 2673, H.Rept. 108-401, filed November 25, 2003), which incorporated seven regular appropriations acts, including Transportation-Treasury appropriations. The conference also dropped two Cuba provisions from the House version of H.R. 2989 that would have eased

---

[50] For a complete listing and discussion of all Cuba bills in the 108th Congress, see CRS Report RL31740, *Cuba: Issues for the 108th Congress*, by Mark P. Sullivan.

restrictions on remittances and on people-to-people educational exchanges. The White House again threatened to veto any legislation that would weaken economic sanctions against Cuba.

The House provisions had been approved during September 9, 2003, House floor consideration of the H.R. 2989: H.Amdt. 375 (Flake), approved by a vote of 227-188, would have prevented funds from enforcing travel restrictions (§745 of the House version); H.Amdt. 377 (Delahunt), approved by a vote of 222-196, would have prevented funds from enforcing restrictions on remittances (§746); and H.Amdt. 382 (Davis), approved by a vote of 246-173, would have prohibited funds from being used to eliminate the travel category of people-to-people educational exchanges (§749).

During Senate floor consideration of H.R. 2989 on October 23, 2003, the Senate approved by voice vote S.Amdt. 1900 (Dorgan), nearly identical to the Flake amendment noted above that would have prevented funds from being used to administer or enforce restrictions on travel or travel-related transactions (§643 of the Senate version). A motion to table the Dorgan amendment was defeated by a vote of 59-36. The Senate approved the bill by a vote of 91-3. The only difference between the Senate and House language was that the Dorgan amendment, as amended by S.Amdt. 1901 (Craig), provided that the section would take effect one day after enactment of the bill.

In other action, the conference on the FY2004 Consolidated Appropriations Act, P.L. 108-199 (H.R. 2673), also dropped a provision in the Senate version of the FY2004 agriculture appropriations bill that would have allowed travel to Cuba under a general license for travel related to the sale of agricultural and medical goods. On July 17, 2003, the Senate Appropriations Committee approved its version of the FY2004 agriculture appropriations bill, S. 1427, that included a provision (§760) allowing travel to Cuba under a general license (which does not require applying to the Treasury Department) for travel related to the commercial sale of agricultural and medical goods. The Senate included this provision when it approved H.R. 2673 on November 6, 2003. The House-passed version of the bill, H.R. 2673, had no such provision. At present, such travel to Cuba is allowed with OFAC's approval of a specific license. In early June 2003, the Treasury Department rejected an application to travel to Cuba for organizers of a second U.S. food and agribusiness fair in Havana.[51] The first such trade fair, held in September 2002, featured some 288 exhibitors from more than 30 states and resulted in millions in U.S. agricultural sales to Cuba.[52]

Second Session Action

Several FY2005 appropriations measures had provisions that would have eased Cuba sanctions, but these were dropped in the FY2005 omnibus appropriations measure (H.R. 4818, H.Rept. 108-792).

The House-passed version of the FY2005 Commerce, Justice, and State appropriations bill, H.R. 4754, approved July 8, 2004 (397-18), included a provision (§801) that would have prohibited funds from being used to implement, administer, or enforce recent amendments to the Cuba embargo regulations that tightened restrictions on gift parcels and baggage taken by individuals

---

[51] Nancy San Martin, "U.S. Pulls Plug on Cuba Expo," *Miami Herald*, June 18, 2003.

[52] Nancy San Martin, "U.S. Official Dampens Trade-Show Enthusiasm with Talks of Cuban Credit," *Miami Herald*, September 29, 2002.

for travel to Cuba. The provision was added by a Flake amendment, H.Amdt. 647, approved by a vote of 221-194 on July 7, 2004. The Senate version of the bill, S. 2809, as reported out of committee, did not include such a provision.

Both the House-approved version of the FY2005 Transportation/Treasury appropriations bill, H.R. 5025, and the Senate Appropriations Committee version of the bill, S. 2806, had provisions that would have eased Cuba sanctions in various ways. In its statement of policy on H.R. 5025, the Administration indicated that the President would veto the measure if it contained provisions weakening Cuba sanctions.

The House-passed version of H.R. 5025 had three provisions that would have eased Cuba sanctions. During floor consideration on September 21, 2004, by a vote of 225-174, the House approved a Davis (of Florida) amendment (H.Amdt. 769), which provided that no funds could be used to administer, implement, or enforce the Bush Administration's June 2004 tightening of restrictions on visiting relatives in Cuba. On September 22, 2004, the House approved two additional Cuba amendments by voice vote, a Waters amendment (H.Amdt. 770) that would have prohibited funds from being used to implement any sanction imposed on private commercial sales of agricultural commodities or medicine or medical supplies to Cuba and a Lee amendment (H.Amdt. 771) that would have prohibited funds from being used to implement, administer, or enforce the Bush Administration's June 2004 tightening of restrictions on travel for educational activities. The House also rejected a Rangel amendment (H.Amdt. 772) on September 22, 2004, by a vote of 225-188 that would have more broadly prohibited funds from being used to implement, administer, or enforce the economic embargo of Cuba. During September 15, 2004, House floor consideration of H.R. 5025, Representative Jeff Flake announced his intention not to offer an amendment, as he had for the past three years, which would have prohibited funds from being used to administer or enforce restrictions on travel or travel-related transactions.

The Senate version of the FY2005 Transportation/Treasury appropriations bill, S. 2806, as reported out of the Senate Appropriations Committee (S.Rept. 108-342) on September 15, 2004, had a provision (§222) that would have prohibited funds from administering or enforcing restrictions on Cuba travel or travel-related transactions. That provision, which was proposed by Senator Byron Dorgan, was unanimously approved by the Subcommittee on Transportation, Treasury, and General Government on September 9, 2004.

The Senate version of the FY2005 Agriculture Appropriation bill, S. 2803, as reported by the Senate Appropriations Committee (S.Rept. 108-340), had a provision (§776) that would have directed the Secretary of the Treasury to promulgate regulations allowing for travel to Cuba under a "general license" when it was related to the commercial sale of agricultural and medical products. The House-passed version of the bill, H.R. 4766, had no such provision. In its statement of policy on the bill, the Administration stated that the President would veto the measure if it contained a provision weakening Cuba sanctions.

Additional Initiatives in the 108th Congress

Among other initiatives introduced in the 108th Congress, but not acted upon, two bills would specifically have lifted restrictions on travel to Cuba: S. 950 (Enzi), introduced April 30, 2003, and H.R. 2071 (Flake), introduced May 13, 2003. H.R. 3422 (Serrano), introduced October 30, 2003, would, among other provisions, have lifted restrictions on travel to Cuba. Three broad legislative initiatives were introduced that would have lifted all Cuba embargo restrictions, including those on travel: H.R. 188 (Serrano), introduced January 7, 2003, S. 403 (Baucus), introduced February 13, 2003, and H.R. 1698 (Paul), introduced April 9, 2003. Another initiative, S. 2449 (Baucus)/H.R. 4457 (Otter), introduced respectively on May 19 and 20, 2004, would have required yearly congressional approval for the renewal of trade and travel restrictions with respect to Cuba. Finally, H.R. 4678 (Davis of Florida), introduced June 24, 2004, in the aftermath of the President's tightening of Cuba sanctions, would have barred certain additional restrictions on travel and remittances to Cuba.

Legislative Initiatives in the 107th Congress[53]

In the 107th Congress, although various measures were introduced that would have eliminated or eased restrictions on travel to Cuba and the House voted in both the first and second sessions to prohibit spending to administer the travel regulations, no legislative action was completed by the end of the second session.

First Session Action

During July 25, 2001, floor action on H.R. 2590, the FY2002 Treasury Department appropriations bill, the House approved an amendment that would prohibit spending for administering Treasury Department regulations restricting travel to Cuba. H.Amdt. 241, offered by Representative Flake (which amended H.Amdt. 240 offered by Representative Smith), would prohibit funding to administer the Cuban Assets Control Regulations (administered by OFAC) with respect to any travel or travel-related transaction. The amendment was approved by a vote of 240 to 186, compared to a vote of 232-186 for a similar amendment in last year's Treasury Department appropriations bill.

The Senate version of H.R. 2590, approved September 19, 2001, did not include any provision regarding U.S. restrictions on travel to Cuba, and the provision was not included in the House-Senate conference on the bill (H.Rept. 107-253). During Senate floor debate, Senator Byron Dorgan noted that he had intended to offer an amendment on the issue, but that he decided not to because he did not want to slow passage of the bill. He indicated that he would support the House provision during conference, but ultimately, however, the House-Senate conference report on the bill did not include the Cuba provision. In light of the changed congressional priorities in the aftermath of the September 11 attacks on New York and Washington, conference negotiators reportedly did not want to slow passage of the bill with any controversial provisions. The Bush Administration had threatened to veto the Treasury bill if it included the Cuba travel provision.

Second Session Action

The Cuba travel issue received further consideration in the second session of the 107th Congress. A bipartisan House Cuba working group of 40 Representatives vowed as one of its goals to work for a lifting of travel restrictions. On February 11, 2002, the Senate Appropriations Committee's Subcommittee on Treasury and General Government held a hearing on the issue, featuring Administration and outside witnesses.

---

[53] For a complete listing and discussion of all Cuba bills in the 107th Congress, see CRS Report RL30806, *Cuba: Issues for the 107th Congress*, by Mark P. Sullivan and Maureen Taft-Morales.

The travel issue was part of debate during consideration of the FY2003 Treasury Department appropriations bill (H.R. 5120 and S. 2740). Secretary of State Colin Powell and Secretary of the Treasury Paul O'Neill said they would recommend that the President veto legislation that includes a loosening of restrictions on travel to Cuba (or a weakening of restrictions on private financing for U.S. agricultural exports to Cuba).[54] The White House also stated that President Bush would veto such legislation.[55]

In July 23, 2002, floor action on H.R. 5120, the House approved three Cuba sanctions amendments, including one on the easing of travel restrictions offered by Representative Jeff Flake. The House approved the Flake travel amendment (H.Amdt. 552), by a vote of 262-167 that would provide that no funds could be used to administer or enforce the Treasury Department regulations with respect to travel to Cuba. The Flake amendment would not prevent the issuance of general or specific licenses for travel to Cuba. Some observers raised the question of whether the effect of this amendment would be limited since the underlying embargo regulations restricting travel would remain unchanged; enforcement action against violations of the relevant embargo regulations could potentially take place in future years when the Treasury Department appropriations measure did not include the funding limitations on enforcing the travel restrictions.[56]

During consideration of H.R. 5120, the House also rejected two Cuba amendments. A Rangel amendment (H.Amdt. 555), rejected by a vote of 204-226, would have prevented any funds in the bill from being used to implement, administer, or enforce the overall economic embargo of Cuba, which includes travel. A Goss amendment (H.Amdt. 551), rejected by a vote of 182-247, would have provided that any limitation on the use of funds to administer or enforce regulations restricting travel to Cuba or travel-related transactions would only apply after the President certified to Congress that certain conditions were met regarding biological weapons and terrorism.[57] The rule for the bill's consideration, H.Res. 488 (H.Rept. 107-585), had provided that the Goss amendment would not be subject to amendment.

The House subsequently passed H.R. 5120 on July 24, 2002, by a vote of 308-121, with the three Cuba amendments, including the Flake Cuba travel amendment.

The Senate version of the Treasury Department appropriations measure, S. 2740, as reported by the Senate Committee on Appropriations on July 17, 2002 (S.Rept. 107-212), included a provision, in Section 516, that was similar, although not identical, to the Flake amendment described above. It provided that no funds may be used to enforce the Treasury Department regulations with respect to any travel or travel-related transactions, but would not prevent OFAC from issuing general and specific licenses for travel to Cuba. In addition, Section 124 of the Senate bill stipulated that no Treasury Department funds for "Departmental Offices, Salaries, and Expenses" may be used by OFAC, until OFAC has certain procedures in place to expedite license applications for travel to Cuba.

---

[54] U.S. Department of State, International Information Programs, Washington File, "Bush Administration Opposes Legislative Efforts to Amend Cuba Policy," July 16, 2002.

[55] White House, Press Briefing by Ari Fleischer, July 24, 2002.

[56] "House Approves Limits on Treasury Enforcement of Cuba Embargo," *Inside U.S. Trade*, July 26, 2002.

[57] For further information on the issues of biological weapons and terrorism as they relate to Cuba, see CRS Report RL30806, *Cuba: Issues for the 107th Congress*, by Mark P. Sullivan and Maureen Taft-Morales.

Congress did not complete action on the FY2003 Treasury Department appropriations measure before the end of the 107th Congress, so action was deferred until the 108th Congress.

Additional Legislative Initiatives in the 107th Congress

Several other initiatives were introduced in the 107th Congress that would have eased U.S. restrictions on travel to Cuba, but no action was taken on these measures.

- H.R. 5022 (Flake), introduced June 26, 2002, would have lifted all restrictions on travel to Cuba.

- Several broad bills would have lifted all sanctions on trade, financial transactions, and travel to Cuba: H.R. 174 (Serrano), the Cuban Reconciliation Act, introduced January 3, 2001, and identical bills S. 400 (Baucus) and H.R. 798 (Rangel), the Free Trade with Cuba Act, introduced February 27 and 28, 2001, respectively.

- S. 1017 (Dodd) and H.R. 2138 (Serrano), the Bridges to the Cuban People Act of 2001, introduced June 12, 2001, would, among other provisions, have removed all restrictions on travel to Cuba by U.S. nationals or lawful permanent resident aliens.

- Several bills would, among other provisions, have repealed the travel restrictions imposed in the 106th Congress by the Trade Sanctions Reform and Export Enhancement Act of 2000 (P.L. 106-387, Title IX, Section 910). These include identical bills S. 402 (Baucus) and H.R. 797 (Rangel), the Cuban Humanitarian Trade Act of 2001, introduced February 27 and 28, 2001; S. 171 (Dorgan), introduced January 24, 2001; and S. 239 (Hagel), the Cuba Food and Medicine Access Act of 2001, introduced February 1, 2001.

Legislative Initiatives in the 106th Congress

The only action completed by the 106th Congress relating to Cuba travel involved a tightening of travel restrictions. The final version of the FY2001 agriculture appropriations measure (P.L. 106-387, Title IX, Trade Sanctions Reform and Export Enhancement Act of 2000) included a provision that restricts travel to Cuba to those categories of non-tourist travel already allowed by the Treasury Department regulations. Section 910 of the law provides that neither general nor specific licenses for travel to Cuba can be provided for activities that do not fit into the 12 categories expressly authorized in the Cuban Assets Control Regulations, Section 515.560 (a) of Title 31, CFR, paragraphs (1) through (12).

As noted in the law, the Secretary of the Treasury may not authorize travel-related transactions "for travel to, from, or within Cuba for "tourist activities," which are defined as any activity that is not expressly authorized in the 12 categories of the regulations. The provision prevents the Administration from loosening the travel restrictions to allow tourist travel. This, in effect, strengthens restrictions on travel to Cuba and somewhat circumscribes the authority of OFAC to issue specific travel licenses on a case-by-case basis under Section 515.560 (b) of Title 31, CFR. OFAC in the past has utilized that section to provide specific licenses for activities that do not fit neatly within the categories of travel set forth in 515.560 (a), including such travel for medical evacuations of Americans legally in Cuba and for U.S. contractors servicing the needs of the U.S.

Interests Section. (Regulations implementing the provision of the law were issued by OFAC on July 12, 2001.)

In other legislative action, the Senate considered the issue of travel to Cuba in June 30, 1999 floor action on the FY2000 Foreign Operations Appropriations bill, S. 1234. An amendment was introduced by Senator Christopher Dodd that would have terminated regulations or prohibitions on travel to Cuba and on transactions related to such travel in most instances.[58] The Senate defeated the amendment by tabling it in a 55-43 vote on June 30, 1999. On November 10, 1999, Senator Dodd introduced identical language as S. 1919, the Freedom to Travel to Cuba Act of 2000, but no action was taken on the bill.

The House took up the issue of travel to Cuba when it considered H.R. 4871, the Treasury Department appropriations bill, on July 20, 2000. A Sanford amendment was approved (232-186) to prohibit funds in the bill from being used to administer or enforce the Cuban Assets Control Regulations with respect to any travel or travel-related transaction. Subsequently, the language of the amendment was dropped from a new version of the FY2001 Treasury Department appropriations bill, H.R. 4985, introduced on July 26. H.R. 4985 was appended to the conference report on the Legislative Branch appropriations bill—H.R. 4516, H.Rept. 106-796—in an attempt to bypass Senate debate on its version of the Treasury appropriations bill, S. 2900. The Senate initially rejected this conference report on September 20, 2000, by a vote of 28-69, but later agreed to the report, 58-37, on October 12. The House had agreed to the conference report earlier, on September 14, 2000, by a vote of 212-209.

Author Contact Information

Mark P. Sullivan
Specialist in Latin American Affairs
msullivan@crs.loc.gov, 7-7689

---

[58] The Dodd amendment allowed for travel restrictions to be imposed if the United States is at war with Cuba, if armed hostilities are in progress, or when threats to physical safety or public health exist. Under current law, the Secretary of State has the same authority to restrict travel (22 USC 211a).